S. Hrg. 113–505

IRRIGATION PROJECTS IN INDIAN COUNTRY

HEARING

BEFORE THE

COMMITTEE ON INDIAN AFFAIRS
UNITED STATES SENATE

ONE HUNDRED THIRTEENTH CONGRESS

SECOND SESSION

SEPTEMBER 10, 2014

Printed for the use of the Committee on Indian Affairs

U.S. GOVERNMENT PRINTING OFFICE

91–750 PDF   WASHINGTON : 2014

For sale by the Superintendent of Documents, U.S. Government Printing Office
Internet: bookstore.gpo.gov   Phone: toll free (866) 512–1800; DC area (202) 512–1800
Fax: (202) 512–2104   Mail: Stop IDCC, Washington, DC 20402–0001

CONTENTS

IRRIGATION PROJECTS IN INDIAN COUNTRY

WEDNESDAY, SEPTEMBER 10, 2014

U.S. SENATE,
COMMITTEE ON INDIAN AFFAIRS,
Washington, DC.

The Committee met, pursuant to notice, at 2:30 p.m. in room 628, Dirksen Senate Office Building, Hon. Jon Tester, Chairman of the Committee, presiding.

OPENING STATEMENT OF HON. JON TESTER, U.S. SENATOR FROM MONTANA

The CHAIRMAN. The Committee will come to order.

Good afternoon to everybody. Today the Committee is holding an oversight hearing on the management of irrigation systems throughout Indian Country. Irrigation systems are vitally important for economic development on a number of reservations in this Country. Often these systems benefit both Indian and non-Indian communities. There are over 100 irrigation systems across Indian Country that are owned and managed by the Department of Interior. These systems range in size, the smallest may focus on only subsistence farming while some of the larger projects can span tens of thousands of acres of critical components for the tribal economies that they serve.

All together, these irrigation systems reach about 1 billion acres, billion with a B. A smaller set of revenue-generating irrigation projects make up the bulk of that acreage, and BIA estimates that the projects lead to about $300 million worth of agricultural crops grown each year.

While these irrigation projects are important to reservation economies, they have been allowed to deteriorate for decades. In 2006, a GAO study found that these projects had hundreds of millions of dollars in deferred maintenance needs. And I can assure you, we have not made much of an investment since 2006.

More recent estimates by the BIA place the maintenance needs at about $600 million. The GAO study also found some issues with staffing levels and the BIA's communication with the irrigation system stakeholders. I look forward to hearing about any improvements that the BIA has made on these issues from both our Federal and our tribal witnesses.

This is not the first time the Committee has looked into this issue. Senator Barrasso presided over a field hearing in Wyoming on this issue last Congress. And from a review of the testimony submitted by witnesses today, it doesn't seem that much has improved. However, I do know that the BIA is taking steps to better assess the unmet needs. Solving the problem is largely an issue of funding, so I am happy to work with my colleagues to find ways to provide the resources to fix and improve and make these irrigation infrastructure projects functional once again.

The Vice Chairman has also expressed interest in this area, with provisions he added to the Authorized Rural Projects Completion Act. The bill was reported out of the ENR Committee last fall and would address funding for both irrigation maintenance and future tribal water settlements.

I want to thank everybody who is going to testify today, especially those who traveled great distances to be here. I appreciate you making that sacrifice. Our tribal witnesses should shed light on how important these irrigation systems are for our communities, and I suspect all the witnesses today will share ideas on how we can address fixing these irrigation systems as we move forward.

Senator Barrasso is not here. When he comes, we will accommodate his opening statement. But for right now, I want to welcome our first witness, Mr. Larry Roberts, who is Principal Deputy Assistant Secretary for Indian Affairs at the Department of Interior. Mr. Roberts, I will remind you and well, before we get to you, we have the honorable Senator from Wyoming here. I will kick it over to you, John, for your opening statement.

STATEMENT OF HON. JOHN BARRASSO, U.S. SENATOR FROM WYOMING

Senator BARRASSO. Thank you, Mr. Chairman. Thank you for holding this important meeting on Indian irrigation.

I want to welcome my friend, Mitch, who is here, a tribal water engineer from the Eastern Shoshone and Northern Arapaho Tribes in Wyoming. I am looking forward to the testimony that you are going to present today. You testified at the field hearing in 2011 in Wyoming in Fremont County, and you are very familiar with the challenges that face irrigation projects, specifically in Wyoming.

There are 16 irrigation projects that were initiated in the late 1800s and early 1900s by the Department of Interior. When they were first built, these Indian irrigation projects were intended to be a central component for the tribal economy. One of those projects is in the Wind River Reservation in my home State of Wyoming. The other irrigation systems are in States of members of this Committee. We have Montana, Washington, Arizona, New Mexico, Idaho.

The Wind River irrigation project, like the 14 other Indian irrigation projects, is "revenue generating," and in theory, is supposed to be self-sustaining. In 2006, the Government Accountability Office found that many of these projects were never completed and are not sustaining themselves. The Committee field hearing held in Wyoming in 2011 confirmed a serious backlog in deferred maintenance that exists and continues to grow.

However, the projects are still a very important source of income and economic development. So Mr. Chairman, the Federal Government's promise to Indian Country to build and maintain these projects needs to be fulfilled.

Last year I offered an amendment to S. 715, the Authorized Rural Water Projects Completion Act, which was pending before the Energy and Natural Resources Committee. That amendment, which was strongly supported by the Committee and the tribes, would provide much-needed assistance for the rehabilitation of Indian irrigation projects. I want to work with you, Mr. Chairman, and the Administration, in continuing to address these serious irrigation issues. The Department of Interior submitted to this Committee an accomplishments report in January of 2013 that summarized several policies established to improve the Indian irrigation program. So I look forward to hearing from the witnesses today on how the Department has implemented the policies and what other improvements are needed to address these important projects.

Thank you, Mr. Chairman.

The CHAIRMAN. Thank you, Senator Barrasso, for your comments.

Mr. Roberts, you and the second panel, I would ask you to hold our comments to about five minutes each, as close to that as you can make it. It will give us an opportunity to ask further questions. Know that you all, all of your full written statements will be a part of the official record. So I want to thank you all again for coming today.

Larry, you may begin.

STATEMENT OF LARRY ROBERTS, PRINCIPAL DEPUTY ASSISTANT SECRETARY, INDIAN AFFAIRS, U.S. DEPARTMENT OF THE INTERIOR

Mr. ROBERTS. Thank you, good afternoon, Chairman Tester, Vice Chairman Barrasso, members of the Committee. My name is Larry Roberts, I am the Principal Deputy Assistant Secretary for Indian Affairs at the Department of Interior. I am a citizen of the Oneida Nation of Wisconsin.

With me today is David Fisher, Chief of our Irrigation and Power Branch. I want to thank you for inviting the Department to provide testimony on irrigation projects in Indian Country. We appreciate the Committee's continued leadership on this issue. It is a daunting challenge, and it is a challenge that is similar to a number of different infrastructure issues we face across the Country.

As the Committee knows, the Federal Government has been involved with Indian irrigation since the Colorado River Indian irrigation project that was authorized in 1867. Today the BIA irrigation program is responsible for oversight and administration of 15 revenue-generating Indian irrigation projects that provide services and deliver water to over 25,000 customers and over 750,000 acres of land in Indian Country.

BIA's irrigation asset inventory includes approximately 6,200 miles of canals and drains and over 58,000 irrigation structures. The asset inventory and program responsibilities also include two BIA-owned facilities at non-revenue generating irrigation projects, including the Navajo Indian irrigation project in New Mexico and the Pyramid Lake irrigation project in northern Nevada.

Historically, the Bureau has not charged sufficient operation and maintenance rehabilitation rates, O&M rates, to allow for adequate project maintenance and replacement. Over time this has resulted in less maintenance accomplished and a steady increase in deferred maintenance. This contributed to the critical reviews by the Office of the Inspector General in the 1990s and the Government Accountability Office in 2006.

In response to these reviews, the Bureau implemented a number of reforms. The BIA has increased the level of engineering and technical support and management oversight for project managers, as recommended by the reports, by putting these projects under the direct supervision of regional or central irrigation office staff or by implementing more stringent protocols for engineering review and approval of actions taken at the projects. BIA is also holding water using meetings at least twice annually. This policy was implemented to solicited input from project stakeholders and provide transparency on the planned use of operation and maintenance funds.

In addition to collecting more feedback on its management performance, BIA is providing more opportunity for direct stakeholder involvement in all or parts of its projects.

And finally, as both Chairman Tester and Vice Chairman Barrasso have mentioned on a number of occasions, the issue of deferred maintenance. As part of our efforts to address that issue, we have been conducting condition assessments. Nearly all of those assessments are completed. We have three remaining assessments that are ongoing. Those are scheduled to be completed in 2017.

So today, some of the 15 revenue-generating Indian irrigation projects operate with annual O&M fees that are near or at the full cost of service. But we believe that rates need to be set at levels to extend the growth of deferred maintenance. But the existing level of deferred maintenance, the existing $600 million backlog that we have, is such that it cannot be economically addressed through increasing O&M rates.

The 2013 deferred maintenance estimate for BIA-owned irrigation facilities is approximately $600 million. We understand this is a longstanding issue and we know that the Department and BIA have worked closely with Committee staff over the years to address the issue. As both of you mentioned today, this Congress has introduced legislation that would provide resources to address the deferred maintenance backlog at many of the BIA irrigation projects. We stand ready to continue our work with the Committee on that legislation.

Many of the key structures still function today. They are the same structures that were constructed over 100 years ago. In spite of their current condition, BIA estimates that irrigated lands served by the 15 BIA revenue-generating irrigation projects had approximately $300 million in revenue and supports almost 10,000 jobs. So with that, I am happy to answer any questions that the Committee may have.

[The prepared statement of Mr. Roberts follows:]

PREPARED STATEMENT OF LARRY ROBERTS, PRINCIPAL DEPUTY ASSISTANT SECRETARY, INDIAN AFFAIRS, U.S. DEPARTMENT OF THE INTERIOR

Good afternoon Chairman Tester, Vice Chairman Barrasso, and members of the Committee. My name is Lawrence Roberts and I am the Principal Deputy Assistant Secretary for Indian Affairs at the Department of the Interior (Department). Thank you for inviting the Department to provide testimony on Irrigation Projects in Indian Country. We appreciate the Committee's continued leadership on this issue, as it is a daunting challenge similar to other infrastructure challenges faced across the Nation.

I will begin with a brief discussion of the history of the Bureau of Indian Affairs (BIA) Irrigation Program, provide an overview of the 17 BIA irrigation projects, and discuss the work BIA has been doing on this issue.

Background

The Federal Government has been involved with Indian irrigation since the Colorado River Indian Irrigation Project was authorized in 1867. In the early 1900s, Congress began authorizing funding for construction of numerous Indian irrigation projects in the western United States. At that time, the Indian Irrigation Service led construction and early administration of the projects. In the late 1930s and through the 1940s, as construction activities wrapped up on most projects, the Indian Irrigation Service ceased to exist and operation and maintenance, referred to hereafter as O&M, was transferred to the BIA, where it continues today. The BIA irrigation program is responsible for oversight and administration of fifteen revenue-generating Indian irrigation projects that provide service and delivers water to over 25,000 customers and 750,000 acres of land in Indian Country. BIA's irrigation asset inventory includes approximately 6,200 miles of canals and drains and over 58,000 irrigation structures. The asset inventory and program responsibilities also include BIA-owned facilities at non-revenue generating irrigation projects, including the Navajo Indian Irrigation Project in New Mexico and Pyramid Lake Irrigation Project in northern Nevada. At these facilities the BIA does not assess O&M charges to irrigators; those charges are instead paid through appropriations or other means. The BIA irrigation program also provides limited support to over 100 irrigation systems that were constructed in the early 1900s, most of which are operated and maintained by tribes.

Overview of the Irrigation Projects in Indian Country

BIA irrigation projects are vital economic contributors to the local communities and regions where they are located. Recent BIA studies show that the irrigation projects in Indian Country are in various states of disrepair. Many of the key structures still functioning today are the same structures that were constructed over 100 years ago. In spite of their current condition, BIA estimates that irrigated lands served by the 15 BIA revenue generating irrigation projects add $490M in revenue and supports almost 10,000 jobs.

The BIA operates its irrigation projects consistent with numerous laws, regulations and policy guidance and many projects have extensive, specific legislative histories. For example, specific statutory authorities require that BIA charge O&M assessments to both Indian and non-Indian customers, and to reimburse the Federal Government for such O&M costs. Most of the 15 revenue-generating projects receive little or no appropriated funds. Whenever possible and practical, BIA works to leverage cost-share opportunities with any other funding that is made available to tribes and water user organizations. BIA increased its funding request in the FY15 President' Budget Request for irrigation project rehabilitation to $2,612,000 from $998,000, an increase of $1,614,000. The appropriated Construction Funds for Indian Irrigation Projects are prioritized using multiple factors, including Critical Health and Safety factors and the Rehabilitation Priority Index (RPI) values determined from the BIA's Condition Assessment process. Projects are submitted from our Regional Office engineers and ranked by our Central Office engineering team using a formal ranking process. Emergency repair situations also come into play given the large deferred maintenance backlog, occasionally requiring the reprogramming of those funds to address those needs. Projects that have received these funds in the past include lining of the Tyhee Siphon, a critical feature for the Fort Hall Project in Idaho; repair of the Two Medicine Canal failure on the Blackfeet Irrigation Project in Montana; and repair of the Dr. Morrison canal failure on the Pine River Irrigation Project in Colorado. We will use this same process for determining the FY15 projects that will be funded. As discussed below, without new funding deferred maintenance remains an enormous challenge.

Historically, BIA has not charged sufficient Operation, Maintenance & Rehabilitation (OM&R) rates to allow for adequate project maintenance and replacement. Over time, this has resulted in less maintenance accomplished and a steady increase in deferred maintenance. This contributed to critical reviews by the Office of Inspector General in the 1990s and the Government Accounting Office in 2006.

Fifteen of the seventeen BIA projects operate with annual O&M fees near or at the full-cost of service. We believe that rates are now set at levels to stem the growth of deferred maintenance, but the existing level of deferred maintenance is such that it cannot be economically addressed through increased O&M rates. Over the past decade or more, BIA has made significant progress in systematically increasing O&M rates at projects where O&M rates are insufficient. In fact, over the past 10 years, O&M rates have increased approximately 29 percent on average at BIA irrigation projects, with one project's rates increased by 74 percent.

Program Accomplishments

The BIA irrigation program has made significant strides over the past eight years in addressing a variety of issues critical to the program. These efforts include setting O&M rates at levels we believe are more sustainable for current operations, and these efforts need to continue in this area to ensure sustainability of operations and maintenance into the future.

There are other Department initiatives BIA is implementing that address challenges at BIA irrigation projects. Some of these initiatives are in response to recommendations by the Department's Office of Inspector General and the GAO. One recommendation made in those reports was that BIA should increase the level of engineering technical support and management oversight for project managers by putting these projects under the direct supervision of regional or central irrigation office staff, or by implementing more stringent protocols for engineering review and approval of actions taken at the projects. In February 2007, BIA established policies to ensure adequate technical oversight and assistance is given to project managers of the BIA irrigation projects.

In addition to these managerial reforms the BIA is working more closely with water users, which include the tribe(s), tribal members, and non-Indians, to be responsive to their concerns and giving the water users a greater role in Project operations.

In July 2006, a policy was established requiring BIA to hold water users meetings at least twice annually. This policy was implemented to solicit input from project stakeholders and provide transparency on the planned use of O&M funds. In addition to collecting more feedback on its management performance, BIA is providing more opportunity for direct stakeholder involvement of all or part of the project. For example, the Wind River Irrigation Project utilizes a Memorandum of Agreement (MOA) with the Crowheart Bench Water Users Association, and a tripartite agreement among the BIA, the LeClair Unit and the Riverton Valley Irrigation District to conduct O&M activities on BIA's behalf.

In 2008, the BIA revised irrigation regulations published in 25 CFR 171, titled "Irrigation Operation and Maintenance." The revision contains two key features that were included to benefit all BIA irrigation projects, Annual Assessment Waivers and Incentive Agreements. The Annual Assessments Waivers are designed to allow for an easy method to waive the O&M assessments if the BIA cannot deliver irrigation water to a customer. Past regulations required BIA to bill the water user and in order to receive a refund, the water user had to formally appeal the bill. The new regulations streamlined that process to minimize administrative requirements for both BIA and the water users. Many BIA projects have lands that have become idle and have not been farmed for many years. To assist the BIA and land owners, and provide incentive to potential lessees to bring these lands back into production, the new regulations allow for Incentive Agreements. Incentive Agreements allow the project to waive the irrigation O&M assessment for up to three years if the landowner or lessee agrees to make improvements to the lands to bring them back into production. These agreements benefit both the land owner and the project by improving land value and increasing Project O&M revenues.

Irrigation Project Condition Assessments

BIA has taken measureable steps to acquire better information about the irrigation projects to better understand the deferred maintenance backlog. Beginning in 2007, as required by the Department and BIA's Asset Management Plans, BIA began conducting engineering condition assessments. Condition assessments identify the costs to repair and replace infrastructure and includes the development of priorities based on health and safety and the asset priority in relation to the overall project. Since 2007, condition assessments have been completed or are currently being conducted for all of BIA's revenue generating irrigation projects. These studies are funded through appropriations to BIA's irrigation program at the national level as opposed to passing this cost on to project irrigators. The remaining three assessments are scheduled to be completed by 2017.

As the remaining condition assessments are completed, BIA's deferred maintenance estimate will more accurately reflect conditions in the field. In our next round of condition assessments we will also include estimates for road crossing and building repairs, which were not evaluated in the initial assessments. As water settlements are implemented, like the Crow Water Rights Settlement Act of 2010 and the Arizona Water Settlement Act of 2004, BIA's estimate of deferred maintenance will become more refined and better estimates of what might be needed should be available.

Where tribes have received water settlement funding for irrigation rehabilitation, infrastructure is being rehabilitated and modernized to provide reliable irrigation service to customers of BIA-owned and operated facilities for years to come. One example of where water settlement funding is providing large-scale capital improvements and rebuilding an old, dilapidated system into a new, state-of-the-art project is in Arizona at BIA's San Carlos Irrigation Project, which serves the Gila River Indian Community.

Addressing Deferred Maintenance

The 2013 deferred maintenance estimate for BIA-owned irrigation facilities is approximately $600 million. The Department understands that the deferred maintenance backlog at Indian irrigation projects is a longstanding issue. As discussed above, we have completed a number of assessments and anticipate completing the last three assessments by 2017. Without significant capital investment, we believe overcoming the deferred maintenance backlog is unachievable given the current agricultural economies of irrigated agriculture in rural Indian Country.

At the Wind River Irrigation Project in Wyoming, for example, the deferred maintenance backlog is approximately $35 million and the project assesses approximately 35,000 acres. Relying solely on O&M revenues would increase costs to such an extent that irrigated agriculture would likely not be economically viable. The Department and BIA worked closely with Committee staff on this issue over the years. This Congress introduced legislation that would provide resources to address the deferred maintenance backlog at many of BIA's irrigation projects. We stand ready to continue our work with the Committee on such legislation.

This concludes my prepared statement. I will be happy to answer any questions you may have.

The CHAIRMAN. Thank you for your testimony, Larry.

We are going to flesh out this O&M fee thing a little more here. If the irrigation systems had no deferred maintenance, if this $600 million, if we spent the $600 million and took care of that backlog, are you saying that the O&M fees that are charged the users right now would cover? Are they adequate to cover any kind of maintenance over the next year?

Mr. ROBERTS. My understanding of the situation is that at some of our projects, those rates are high enough. But if Congress were to pass legislation to affect the deferred maintenance issue, our goal would be to have all of those O&M fees basically be self-sustaining. So it is a careful balance, because obviously we want the farms and farmers to be economically viable. The goal is to have those rates reflect actual O&M costs. We are there at some of the projects right now.

The CHAIRMAN. We are there with some of the projects and not with others?

Mr. ROBERTS. That is right.

The CHAIRMAN. Do you have the information to be able to do that, to know what to set those O&M fees at? And as long as I am talking, all the projects, small ones, big ones?

Mr. ROBERTS. My understanding of the larger projects, there are 17 projects that the Bureau runs. There is another 100 plus projects that the Bureau does not run on a daily basis, those are run by tribes or water authorities. So with the 17 projects, we have done an analysis in terms of how much those rates would need to be. I think those rates, quite frankly, would probably need for some of the projects to be implemented over time.

The CHAIRMAN. Yes.

Mr. ROBERTS. But I think that S. 715 also talked about implementing that maintenance over time as well. So that is sort of our goal, is when we are going to, if such legislation were to be enacted into law, that we don't want to end up in the same place we are right now.

The CHAIRMAN. Okay. Governor Paisano of the Sandia Pueblo will testify that the Pueblos in his area get their water from a Bureau of Rec' owned irrigation system that BIA pays a local conservation district to provide sufficient amounts of water for the Pueblos' needs. So we have two Federal agencies involved in trust responsibilities for the Pueblos, yet Governor Paisano's testimony says that they are treated worse than any other water users on the system. Are you familiar with this?

Mr. ROBERTS. I am familiar with the issue. I know that Assistant Secretary Washburn and more specifically, Director Mike Black, have been personally involved in those conversations, in negotiating O&M rates. We do have responsibilities there with all the Pueblos. Quite frankly, in those negotiations, my understanding is that we have withheld payment because we were basically advocating for the tribal rights there, and wanting those O&M rates to be set appropriately. So those conversations are ongoing and Director Mike Black is personally involved in those.

The CHAIRMAN. You are dealing with the Bureau of Rec.

Mr. ROBERTS. Bureau of Rec, but we are also dealing with the Middle Rio Grande Water District that we contract with.

The CHAIRMAN. Okay. So do you have the ability to require those folks to treat folks equally? The conservation district in particular.

Mr. ROBERTS. We have to get to a fair rate on O&M costs. And like I said, I know that we have withheld payments. And we are in active negotiations right now. So it is a complicated issue. We are working with them and like I said, I think Director Black has spent a lot of time on this issue personally.

The CHAIRMAN. Do you consult with tribes on their funding priorities?

Mr. ROBERTS. We do.

The CHAIRMAN. So where are irrigation projects? When you do your consultation, are they on the list, number one, and where are they if they are?

Mr. ROBERTS. We consult with tribes through the tribal budget committee that the Department of Interior has. All regions are represented there. It is an issue that is raised. We have 17 facilities, so it doesn't impact every tribe like for example education, law enforcement, social services. So it is a priority. I don't know that it is the top priority that we hear from Indian Country.

The CHAIRMAN. But it is a priority, and the Department knows it is a priority for the tribes?

Mr. ROBERTS. Yes, Senator.

The CHAIRMAN. Senator Barrasso?

Senator BARRASSO. Thank you, Mr. Chairman.

Mr. Roberts, during recent drought years, the irrigation system operated by the Bureau of Indian Affairs on the Wind River Reservation experienced significant water shortages. In some cases, the agency had to shut offer water to several users.

Meanwhile, same time, the neighboring Crowheart Irrigation System managed by the water users themselves, they appear to have done well during the drought, handled it much more efficiently. Could you explain what the Bureau of Indian Affairs is doing to improve management of the irrigation system so that all water users can continue to access water even during droughts? There is an interesting difference between Crowheart versus BIA.

Mr. ROBERTS. Yes. My understanding of that situation with Crowheart is that that is in a separate drainage and that drainage had more storage there for that year, whereas, I think there were other drainages that didn't have as much storage capacity. But I think there were also issues with other drainages where essentially, some of the diversions that ultimately fed into those drainages had issues related to a pipeline. So there is a pipeline crossing one of the drainages that we were concerned about sending too much water and that that water would hit that crossing pipeline.

So my understanding is that the BIA is working with the tribal water utility during the off-season here to move that pipeline so that it is not an issue, and that we will be able to send more water to some of those areas where we haven't. But I think ultimately, at least on some of those, it was limited storage capacity that led to that.

Senator BARRASSO. On the next panel, we are going to hear from Mitch Cottenoir, from Fremont County in Wyoming. According to his written testimony, little has changed on the Wind River Irrigation Project since the Committee's 2011 field hearing. He specifically notes that the BIA does not have a long-term plan for rehabilitation of this project. The Bureau of Indian Affairs Irrigation Program Overview dated January 3rd of last year, of 2013, cites persistent drought, water availability and tribal politics as unique challenges for this project.

So can you talk a little about how these unique challenges prohibit the agency from developing a long-term rehab plan? And when will you provide this Committee with a long-term plan for addressing the deferred maintenance for the Wind River irrigation project?

Mr. ROBERTS. In terms of a long-term plan addressing deferred maintenance, I think at this point, as I said, it is not a situation where we are going to be able to address it through raising O&M rates. It is a situation where we are able to stem some of the deferred maintenance through O&M rates now, but we are not able to do that with the current funding that we receive. So some of the things that we are doing, we see more droughts, we see more extreme weather conditions, we see more issues not only related to water delivery but other areas on Indian reservations. And so part of what we are doing is working with tribes to help develop that capacity in terms of dealing with those extreme weather events. The other thing that we are doing is we are working with the California Poly Irrigation Training and Research Center and we recently provided training at Wind River to better measure water, so that we have a more accurate read of the water in the system and make better use of that.

So in terms of a, to get back to your final question about a long-term plan, Senator, I don't know that we have that plan, that we have a time frame for that plan. I think what we would want to do is finish all of the assessments. We have three more to finish by the end of 2017. That is our estimated time frame. And from there, we will have a much better sense of the overall deferred maintenance.

Senator BARRASSO. Thank you. Thank you, Mr. Chairman.

The CHAIRMAN. Senator Udall?

STATEMENT OF HON. TOM UDALL, U.S. SENATOR FROM NEW MEXICO

Senator UDALL. Thank you, Chairman Tester. I really appreciate your attention to this.

I believe I told your office, Mr. Roberts, about an urelated question that I wanted to ask about. Because we have you here today, I want to just take a moment to bring up an unrelated issue that has recently come to my attention. It is my understanding that the K–12 Pinehill Schools in the Ramah Navajo Chapter have a heightened fire risk as a result of non-working fire alarms, sprinkler systems and smoke detectors. These life and safety hazards have been allowed to persist. It is unacceptable; it puts the lives of children and their education and adults at serious risk. It is contrary to BIE's own policies and procedures.

It is my understanding that Pine Hill's BIA elementary school that was constructed three years ago was never issued a final certificate of occupancy because it never had a working fire alarm. As a result, this new school has never opened. Again, the waste and lack of attention to vital safety concerns is unacceptable.

I would ask Mr. Roberts and his team to look into these outstanding issues at Pine Hill and expedite steps to put in place these very simple but important safety measures.

My question is, Pine Hill schools are not on the priority list of BIA school facilities in poor condition needing renovation or replacement. Yet there are life safety issues at its schools, including non-working fire alarms and sprinkler systems, certificates of occupancy taking months if not years to be issued, delaying the use of needed facilities. What steps will the BIA take right now to remedy these situations at BIA grant schools like Pinehill?

Mr. ROBERTS. Thank you, Senator. I do know that our staff is working with your staff on this issue and we appreciate that.

In terms of life safety issues with the school that you raise, that is of utmost concern to us. My understanding is that the southwest region does have a contract in place to address the fire alarm issue at that school, which is I guess campus-wide. And then you mentioned the new elementary school that's been constructed. My understanding is that we contracted with the tribe's school district for that construction and that it is 98 percent complete. We are working with the tribe's school board to bring that to full completion. So this is an issue that I will raise both with director Monty Roessell when I get back today and make sure that, obviously, the safety issue there on fire alarms we want to get fixed immediately.

And this issue about construction, I think we need to figure out, since the tribe has contracted for that function, how to get that one across the finish line. My understanding is that it is about 98 percent complete.

Senator UDALL. Thank you very much. This issue has been lingering for a long time. It has been out there. So I think we really need to get expedited attention to it, and I appreciate your attention to it.

Thank you, Chairman.

The CHAIRMAN. Senator Udall, did you just say that they built a new school, didn't finish for three years and it is not open because they don't have a fire alarm system in it?

Senator UDALL. That is right. That is exactly what I said.

The CHAIRMAN. We will have a hearing on this if you guys don't fix it. It should have been done three years ago. I mean, truthfully, this is the kind of stuff that gives government a bad name.

Mr. ROBERTS. I agree.

The CHAIRMAN. Senator Fischer isn't here, but I have some more questions on irrigation. The BIA oversees almost all those Indian irrigation systems. The BOR has some irrigation systems, too. Do you know if the BOR backlog is equivalent to or similar to what the BIA backlog is?

Mr. ROBERTS. I don't know. That is information, Senator, that I can provide to the Committee. My understanding of BOR is that they construct the irrigation project then they turn it over, they don't operate it actually. So I don't know whether they have the same O&M issue or not. But that is something that I will certainly follow up with the Bureau of Reclamation and provide that information to the Committee.

The CHAIRMAN. Okay. Thank you for that.

Many of the recent water settlements authorized tribes to use the Self-Determination Act contracts to manage many aspects of the water infrastructure construction projects. However, a lot of these projects are overseen by Reclamation rather than the BIA. The Crow chairman who is sitting pretty darned close to you is going to testify that Reclamation has required the tribe to use their own funds and then get reimbursed, and this creates a burden, because there is not a lot of extra bucks flowing around. And it is contrary to the Self-Determination Act.

Just a question for you, you have to speak for the Department, but why would the Department of the Interior refuse to comply with the Indian Self-Determination Act?

Mr. ROBERTS. Chairman, I am not up to speed on the specifics of Reclamation's work with the Crow Tribe. But that is something that I can, information that we can provide to the Committee. I don't know if there were specific instances there or not. But is information I would be happy to provide.

The CHAIRMAN. I would appreciate it if you would pass that on, Larry. And then the last question that I have is, have any of the tribes assumed management of the irrigation projects in part or in whole?

Mr. ROBERTS. I know that the Duck Valley Shoshone Paiute Tribe, they have compacted to run the project there.

The CHAIRMAN. Are there any others that come to mind?

Mr. ROBERTS. San Carlos may have as well. But I would have to double check that.

The CHAIRMAN. So when they did the contract, was there a lot of deferred maintenance on those when they did the compact?

Mr. ROBERTS. I think for Duck Valley, their deferred maintenance was addressed in large part through their water settlement.

The CHAIRMAN. Okay. I was just trying to see if I could get any comparison between tribally-compacted irrigation systems and their deferred maintenance versus the ones that the BIA oversees. But I want to make sure we are comparing apples to apples.

Mr. ROBERTS. We can ask our staff to follow up with the Committee on that to see if there are any others that I am just not thinking of.

The CHAIRMAN. I appreciate your work, Larry, in the Department. I appreciate your work with the irrigation systems. I think you understand how important they are to the economy, and you also understand if we lose this infrastructure, it is more costly to get back. The maintenance issue is big.

And I don't mean to be too hard on you on the school thing. If it is our fault, if there is something we haven't done, that stops you from fixing that, then let us know and we will fix it. But if it isn't, then you can move on. You don't need to respond to that. Thank you very much.

I am going to welcome our second panel up as Larry gathers up his papers. I appreciate you making the trek over.

And on our second panel, we are going to have Chairman Old Coyote, Darrin Old Coyote, from the Crow Tribe of Montana. We are then going to hear from Governor Stuart Paisano of the Sandia Pueblo Tribe of New Mexico. Then we have Ruth Jim, Councilwoman from the Yakama Nation of Washington State. Finally, we are going to hear from Mitchell Cottenoir, an engineer with the Shoshone and Arapaho Tribes of the Wind River Reservation that Senator Barrasso talked about. I want to thank you all for being in front of us today. I would remind you to keep your statements to five minutes; it would be very, very much appreciated. It will allow time for questions.

Senator Udall, did you want to introduce Governor Paisano?

Senator UDALL. Yes, I would like to introduce Governor Paisano, if that is okay.

The CHAIRMAN. You bet.

Senator UDALL. Thank you, Chairman Tester. I will save any other comments for later.

But first of all, this is tremendously important to the tribes in my State, what you are holding this hearing on, the irrigation infrastructure. And it is something that is often neglected. I really appreciate you making sure that this isn't overlooked.

I would like to welcome to the Committee my good friend Governor Stuart Paisano. He is the Governor of Sandia Pueblo and Chairman of the Coalition of Six Middle Rio Grande Pueblos. Governor Paisano has served in Pueblo leadership for many years. He was first appointed as Governor in 2000, the youngest ever governor to represent the Pueblo. As Governor of Sandia, Governor Paisano represents a long history of farmers who rely on the Rio Grande for maintaining crop land in our arid State. The Governor can speak to the specific needs of members of his Pueblo who are dealing with crumbling irrigation infrastructure, and can also speak to the difficulty Sandia Pueblo has working with local entities and the BIA, so that the deliveries of the tribe's senior water rights are carried out.

As Chairman of the Coalition of Six Middle Rio Grande Pueblos, Governor Paisano understands the larger issues that confront the six Pueblos who depend on the Middle Rio Grande for community agriculture. The Governor knows the challenges the River Pueblos face working with local conservation and irrigation districts and the need for funding Pueblo infrastructure. After years of drought and centuries of compact negotiation and water lawsuits, water is no simple issue for New Mexico.

I look forward to the Governor's testimony, and look forward to working more with him to address the issues that Sandia Pueblo and the other Rio Grande Pueblos face.

Thank you, Senator Tester.

The CHAIRMAN. Thank you, Senator Udall.

Chairman Old Coyote, you may begin.

STATEMENT OF HON. DARRIN OLD COYOTE, CHAIRMAN, CROW NATION

Mr. OLD COYOTE. Good afternoon, Chairman Tester, Vice Chairman Barrasso and members of the Committee.

Thank you for holding this hearing on irrigation projects in Indian Country. This is an important subject for not only the Crow people but for Indian Country in general.

My name is Darrin Old Coyote and I am the Chairman of the Crow Nation. I am honored to be here on behalf of the Crow Nation to testify on our experiences with the Crow Irrigation Project, or the CIP. I would like to provide the Committee with a summary of the historic issues we experienced with our irrigation system, what has been done and what is being done in the future to achieve a well-run and efficient irrigation system.

The CIP is located on the Crow Indian Reservation in south central Montana and has been a subject of problems for many decades. Construction on the CIP began in the late 1800s, and currently consists of 11 units with a total area of over 60,000 acres. Historically the CIP was operated and maintained by the BIA, who spent the majority of the operation and maintenance budget on personnel costs rather than actual maintenance on the system.

The CIP was also underfunded, because the BIA failed to collect assessments from users of the system. Together, the deferred maintenance and underfunding resulted in a very run-down and inefficient irrigation system. The historical problems at the CIP led to rehabilitation and improvement of the system being a major component of the Crow Tribe Water Rights Settlement Act of 2010. The Crow Water Settlement otherwise, $132 million for CIP rehab, of this amount $74 million was mandatory appropriations.

We cannot emphasize enough the importance of this mandatory funding that was only possible because of Chairman Tester's and Senator Baucus's diligent efforts to find funding offsets. We would like to thank both of them for their hard work on behalf of the Crow Nation. We recommend that future Indian water rights settlements include mandatory funding as well.

The CIP project also requires ongoing annual appropriations to maintain the construction schedule that we are finalizing with

BOR. Most if not all current and future Indian water settlements have a similar annual appropriations need. We urge Congress to continue to appropriate all the necessary funds to complete the critical work on the CIP.

Another aspect of our settlement that benefits the CIP is the provision that allows for flexibility in the transfer of funds between two large construction project accounts: the CIP and the MR&I Clean Drinking Water System. We have already noticed the benefits of carving this type of flexibility into legislation and recommend that future Indian water settlements include such provisions.

The settlement also established BOR as the lead Federal agency, rather than the BIA. In 2011, we entered into a 638 agreement with BOR to carry out the rehabilitation improvement activities. While the tribe supported BOR serving as the lead on the CIP moving forward, we have experienced early obstacles. In fiscal year 2012, there seemed to be very little oversight from BOR before the agency abruptly increased oversight in 2013 and crippled the project's progress. This inconsistent oversight by BOR halted funding to the tribe from March 2013 to January 2014, and caused construction crew layoffs for the entire construction season. The BOR also demanded that the tribe advance construction funds from the tribe's general fund account and seek reimbursement. This is impossible for any tribe.

After difficult discussions and negotiations with BOR, we have evolved to today's level of oversight that is a happy medium and have worked out a funding mechanism that does not require the tribe to advance the construction costs from our general fund budget. Despite these initial obstacles, construction commenced on the CIP in 2012 and we are now in a position to move forward aggressively to rehab the CIP. One of the benefits of funding irrigation projects is that the results are tangible. You can see the before and after pictures of the difference that Federal dollars make on the ground.

Forty jobs will be created in 2015 and we will continue to increase the number of local jobs for the next 10 years. In closing, every Indian irrigation system is unique and poses its own challenges. In our case, we are dealing with several decades of deferred maintenance on the CIP that must be remedied on a strategic, forward-thinking approach in order to make the most out of the Crow water settlement funds. Even though we have experienced a few temporary setbacks in implementation of the settlement, we are headed in the right direction and are optimistic that we will be successful in restoring the CIP.

Thank you again for the opportunity to provide testimony today. I am happy to answer any questions that the Committee may have.

[The prepared statement of Mr. Old Coyote follows:]

PREPARED STATEMENT OF HON. DARRIN OLD COYOTE, CHAIRMAN, CROW NATION

I. Introduction

Good afternoon. My name is Darrin Old Coyote and I am the Chairman of the Crow Nation. On behalf of the Crow Nation, I would like to thank Chairman Tester and members of the Senate Committee on Indian Affairs for holding this Oversight Hearing on Irrigation Projects in Indian Country and inviting the Tribe to provide testimony on our experience with the Crow Irrigation Project within the Crow Reservation.

As I will discuss in further detail below, the Crow Irrigation Project (''CIP'') has been the subject of considerable problems on the Crow Reservation for many decades. Historically, the CIP was operated and maintained by the Bureau of Indian Affairs (''BIA''), with a majority of the Operation and Maintenance (''O&M'') budget weighted towards personnel costs and deferred maintenance that resulted in extensive deficiencies with the CIP. Funding problems were compounded by a failure to collect assessments from users of the system, which left the system seriously underfunded. Thus, in an effort to remedy the vast failings of the CIP, the Crow Tribe Water Rights Settlement of 2010 was enacted to, among other things, rehabilitate and improve the CIP and provide meaningful Federal funding for such work. Today, we share our experience both in terms of the historic issues that have surrounded the CIP, as well as our current and future work with the Department of Interior through the Bureau of Reclamation as it has evolved since passage of the Crow Water Settlement legislation.

II. Brief Overview of Crow Irrigation Project

A. Brief History of Crow Irrigation Project

The CIP is located on the Crow Reservation in south-central Montana. The Crow Tribe's first reservation, established in the Fort Laramie Treaty of 1851, was 35 million acres of land in Montana and Wyoming. In the Fort Laramie Treaty of 1868, the Crow Tribe agreed to reside on an 8-million acre reservation in south-central Montana and established the senior tribal water right claim of the Crow Tribe on May 7, 1868. Later land cessions from the Crow Tribe to the United States in 1882, 1891, and 1904 reduced the Reservation to its current 2.3 million acre size today. Importantly, each land cession and subsequent land sale by the United States to meet its treaty obligations to the Crow Tribe constituted the original and early subsequent appropriations for the Federal CIP.

In 1920, Congress passed the Crow Allotment Act, which triggered a massive land conversion from collective tribal to individual allotted Crow. The amount of land and the number of individual Crow allottees both doubled within fifteen years of this Act. However, for reasons outside of this testimony and despite a federal prohibition on the amount of acreage to ever be owned by a non-Indian individual (1,280 acres) or a corporation (1,920 acres), hundreds of thousands of acres ultimately passed to non-Indians within the Crow reservation. That historical fact, the legal issues, and claims associated with the lands subject to the 1920 Act remain in dispute to the present day. See 1920 Crow Allotment Act, Section 2, 41 Stat. 751 (1920); *Crow Tribe v. Campbell Farming Corp.,* 31 F.3d 768 (9th Cir. 1994).

The first irrigation works, the Reno Ditch, was constructed by the Federal Government in 1885. Surveys for the present CIP began in 1890. The first general authorization for the construction of the irrigation project on the Crow Reservation was contained in the agreement between the Crow Tribe and the United States, dated December 8, 1890, and ratified by Section 31 of the Indian Appropriation Act of March 3, 1891 (26 Stat. 989, I Kappler 407, 432). Designs, surveys, and construction for the CIP were performed by the United States Reclamation Service, now the Bureau of Reclamation (Reclamation), for the BIA until 1922. Reclamation constructed nine of the eleven units from 1885 to 1922. Further construction on the irrigation units was performed by the BIA after 1922. The remaining two irrigation units were privately constructed, with lateral ditches off of the main canals constructed by Reclamation in the early 1920s to serve Crow allotted lands. Active expansion of the irrigation units ceased in 1925 and nearly all of the irrigation facilities were completed before 1940.

Subsequent Congressional acts provided for continued construction and development on the CIP. The Act of July 1, 1932 repealed collection of construction costs against Indian owned lands under government irrigation projects until the land is no longer under Indian ownership. Public Law 79–468 (60 Stat. 333), Section 9 states, ''[n]o further construction work on the Crow Indian Reservation shall be undertaken by the United States without the prior consent of: (1) the Crow Tribe; (2) the irrigation district or districts affected, and; (3) the Congress of the United States, and without the prior execution of repayment contracts by non-Indian water users or irrigation district or districts, obligating the non-Indian lands for the repayment for their share of such construction costs.'' Public Law 79–468 further states, ''that such consent shall not be necessary to construct laterals necessary to irrigate the lands within the CIP as now determined and classified as irrigable by the land designation committee report, as approved by the Secretary of the Interior in 1944.'' The Public Law also cancelled all back debt to the United States government owed by all Indian owned land and also cancelled United States government debt to the Crow Tribe for funds expended from treaty settlements for the irrigation projects.

B. CIP Overview

The Crow Irrigation Project consists of eleven units with a total area of 63,365 acres. There are eleven diversion dams, one storage dam, nine canal systems and five drainage systems. Specifically, the eleven CIP irrigation units consist of the Bighorn, Agency, Forty Mile, Reno, Lodge Grass #1, Lodge Grass #2, Bozeman Trail, Upper Little Horn (Wyola), Pryor, Soap Creek, and Two Leggins Units. The Upper Little Horn Unit is also referred to as Wyola throughout as attributed to the fact that Wyola is the more common name used. Of these eleven units, the Bozeman Trail and Two Leggins Units are privately owned and operated, with the remaining nine CIP Units operated and maintained by the BIA's office located in Crow Agency, Montana. The rehabilitation and betterment of the Bozeman Trail and Two Leggins Units will only occur where land is held in Trust by the United States for the Tribe and Crow Allottees are beneficiaries.

The CIP lands are located along the Bighorn and the Little Bighorn Rivers, Pryor Creek, Lost Creek, Sunday Creek, Soap Creek, and Lodge Grass Creek, all of which are tributaries to the Yellowstone River. The eleven units are located entirely in the Pryor, Lower Bighorn, and Little Bighorn Sub-basins, with the general direction of flow within both basins from southwest to northeast. Across the eleven units, the CIP consists of eleven diversion dams, one storage dam with a capacity of about 23,000 acre-feet, approximately 122 miles of main canals, 43 miles of drains, 257 miles of additional canals (e.g., laterals, sublaterals, and wasteways), and approximately 3,800 irrigation structures (including both BIA and non-BIA-owned structures) such as checks, drops, headworks, flumes, siphons, turnouts, road crossings, spillways, and diversion dams. All units are gravity fed and lack any automated flow measurement or gate controls, with the exception of the Bighorn Unit, which has automated gates controlled by Reclamation at the main diversion point (headworks) at the Afterbay below the Yellowtail Dam and Bighorn Reservoir.

In 2006, the CIP served approximately 1,118 water users. Current irrigation practices include both surface and sprinkler methods, with most irrigation methods consisting of flood, furrow, wheel-lines, gated pipe, and sprinklers with both unlined and lined ditches as distribution systems. Additionally, several select laterals and sublaterals have been converted to pipe, particularly in the Two Leggins Unit. The CIP serves both Tribal and non-Tribal landowners. Non-Tribal landowners in the two irrigation districts (Bighorn and Little Bighorn Districts) and private ditch companies (Bozeman and Two Leggins) in the CIP are organized as legal entities under Montana statutes. The Irrigation District Boards are chartered under state law and only represent owners of fee simple lands.

Most of the reservation is comprised of grasslands and plains with the Wolf Mountains to the east and Bighorn and Pryor Mountains to the southwest. The climate on the reservation varies from humid above 7,000 feet in the Bighorn Mountains, with 24 inches of annual precipitation, to semi-arid around 2,900 feet near Hardin, with 12 inches of annual precipitation. The primary source of water for the CIP originates on Tribal lands in the Bighorn Mountains. All CIP irrigation water is supplied by surface water sources. The primary irrigated crops are hay and alfalfa, irrigated pasture, sugar beets, corn, and grains. Precipitation averages 12–18 inches annually, with temperatures that vary from -48 to +110 degrees Fahrenheit, and the average growing season is 135 days from mid-May to the end of September.

Over the years, the Tribe asserted that the BIA's role in overseeing and maintaining the CIP fell short of the United States' trust obligation to the Tribe and Crow allottees to maintain the system. We saw that the vast majority of funds on the CIP were weighted towards personnel costs rather than much needed O&M. Most recently, for example, there has only been one BIA operator for the entire CIP system who performs such operations with 25 year-old equipment. Accordingly, the CIP continued to wear down and operate at a sub-optimal efficiency level. Indeed, the dilapidated conditions on the CIP spurred the Tribe's efforts to ultimately settle the Tribe's claims against the United States for failing to fulfill its trust obligations to the Tribe, and which resulted in the Crow Tribe Water Rights Settlement Act of 2010.

III. Crow Tribe Water Rights Settlement

The Montana Reserved Water Rights Compact Commission was established by the Montana legislature in 1979 for purposes of concluding compacts for the equitable division and apportionment of waters between the State and its peoples and the Indian Tribes claiming reserved water rights within the State. In 1999, the Montana State Legislature ratified the Crow Tribe-Montana Water Compact. MCA

85–20–901 (1999). By entering into this Compact, all interested parties settled their claims with the State of Montana and the Crow Tribe and avoided costly and lengthy litigation.

In 2010, the United States Congress passed the Crow Tribe Water Rights Settlement Act which further authorized, ratified and confirmed the Crow Tribe-Montana Water Rights Compact entered into by the Tribe and the State of Montana in 1999, and was signed into law by President Obama on December 8, 2010. Claims Resolution Act, P.L. 111–29, Title IV, 124 Stat. 3097 (''Crow Water Settlement''). One of the critical components of the Crow Water Settlement was Interior's obligation to fulfill its trust obligation to properly maintain the CIP, which the Tribe asserted the United States had failed to do. The Crow Water Settlement specifically provided for Reclamation to carry out such activities as necessary to rehabilitate and improve the water diversion and delivery features of the CIP, in accordance with an agreement to be negotiated between the Secretary of Interior and the Crow Tribe. Crow Water Settlement, Sec. 405. In 2011, the Tribe and Reclamation entered into a Self-Determination Contract, commonly referred to as a 638 contract, to carry out the rehabilitation and improvement activities envisioned by the Crow Water Settlement.

Significantly, the Crow Water Settlement also authorized \$132 million, adjusted to reflect changes since May 1, 2008, in construction cost indices applicable to the types of construction involved in the rehabilitation and improvement of the CIP. Of that authorized amount, \$73, 843,000 was a mandatory appropriation, with the remaining \$58,000,000 as authorized discretionary funds. Crow Water Settlement, Sec. 414(a). We cannot emphasize enough the importance of the mandatory funding that was included in our Settlement, which was a direct result of Chairman Tester and former Senator Baucus' diligent efforts to find funding offsets. As you are keenly aware, the mandatory appropriations provide direct funding to enable the Tribe to begin work immediately on the CIP. That being said, it has been emphasized that the discretionary portion of the BIA irrigation funding, approximately \$8 million per year, will need to be substantially increased in the upcoming fiscal years to avoid layoffs and cyclical employment.

Notwithstanding the anticipated increase in construction costs as the project progresses, the mandatory funding element of the Settlement is critical towards the overall intent and success of the Settlement. Thus, while we recognize that identifying offsets and providing for mandatory funding in Indian Water Settlements is a difficult task to say the least, we highly recommend that future Indian water settlements strive to include mandatory funding. We also urge Congress not to forget that the mandatory funding for our and other Indian water settlements will run out and we will need Congress to be prepared to appropriate the funds necessary to complete the critical work of our settlement, including our work on the CIP.

Lastly, with respect to the Crow Water Settlement legislation itself, we were able to include a provision within the Settlement that allowed for flexibility between our two large construction projects—the CIP and the MR&I System (clean drinking water system). Section 414(h) provides that the Secretary of Interior may transfer funds between the CIP account and the MR&I account as the Secretary, with the concurrence of the Tribe, determines to be necessary. We have already noticed the benefits of carving this type of flexibility into the legislation, which in our case was especially important as we work to rehabilitate the existing CIP system and construct a new MR&I System within the Crow Reservation. Again, we would recommend that future Indian water settlements consider such provisions in their settlements if they envision needing a certain level of flexibility between their relevant construction activities.

IV. Current and Future Outlook for the CIP

The Crow Water Settlement provides much needed funding and directives to Reclamation to carry out the necessary construction to improve the overall efficiency of the CIP. Unlike the historical management of the CIP by the BIA, the Crow Water Settlement provided that Reclamation would serve as the lead agency on the project going forward. While the Tribe certainly supported Reclamation serving as the lead on the CIP moving forward, we have experienced early obstacles (perhaps due to an expected learning curve by Reclamation with Indian irrigation projects as opposed to their standard non-Indian projects), both in terms of the level and balance of BOR oversight on the project, as detailed below.

Once construction and improvement continues we expect that project-wide efficiency of the irrigation system to the farm turnouts will be roughly 30 percent. Moreover, future irrigation water demands should decrease from the current existing irrigation system demands with improved system efficiency resulting from rehabilitation and betterment efforts. Efficiencies of 50–70 percent could potentially be realized through a combination of CIP rehabilitation and betterment efforts and improved system O&M. CIP rehabilitation and betterment, in conjunction with improved O&M, may also help to increase irrigation wastewater quality by decreasing pollutant concentrations within the system (e.g., sediments, chemicals, etc.). Reductions in water pollutant concentrations in wastewater ultimately, however, will be largely dependent on individual on-farm irrigation methods and practices.

The total irrigated acres may increase if additional acres currently in TNA (Temporarily Non-Assessed Acres, which are currently not receiving water for various reasons) status can be brought into PA (Presently Assessed acres) status. Currently 8,200 acres of land are identified as TNA. Some of these tracts of land have potential to be irrigated and assessed with minor rehabilitation. The addition of on-farm improvements in other areas may also add more irrigated land, as would the development of additional lands for irrigation (Dunmore Bench).

A. CIP 638 Contract

As discussed above, the Crow Tribe entered into a 638 Contract with Reclamation to implement the CIP. In the first two years of the Settlement Act implementation, we experienced inconsistent oversight, both from the Tribe's perspective and Reclamation's perspective (as referenced above), that resulted in minimal funding to the Tribe from March 2013 to January 2014 and that caused construction crew layoffs for the entire irrigation season. In contrast, FY 2012 seemed to have very little oversight from Reclamation, and then an abrupt change occurred that resulted in significant Reclamation oversight—thus crippling the project's movement. Fortunately, after difficult discussions and negotiations, we have evolved to today's level of oversight that is a happy median, which we believe will lead to successful interactions with Reclamation in the future.

Additionally, the Tribe encountered another substantial obstacle during this first phase of implementation under the 638 Contract when Reclamation demanded that the Tribe advance the funds for construction from the Tribe's general government operating fund (approximately $20 million per year) and be reimbursed after each Reclamation audit. As would undoubtedly be the case for many tribal budgets, this became impossible for the Tribe (it would have caused other tribal department shutdowns and layoffs to provide the advance funding for the water projects). We voiced these concerns with Reclamation and ultimately worked out a mechanism in which the Tribe will no longer have to advance the funds from the Tribe's general fund. Hence, this year's 2015 Annual Funding Agreement (AFA) appears to be on track and we are optimistic that the following important milestones will be achieved.

1. Crow Irrigation Project Master Plan

The 638 Contract executed by the Tribe and Reclamation in 2011 included a requirement that the parties draft a CIP Master Plan of project construction activities and responsibilities under the Contract. The Final Draft CIP Master Plan was reviewed by Reclamation and the BIA, with all final comments received on August 29, 2014. The Final CIP Master Plan was submitted to Reclamation last week for final review and acceptance.

It is anticipated that Reclamation will provide a formal response to the Final CIP Master Plan in the form of a letter, and provided that no additional comments warranting revision in the Master Plan are supplied, the Final CIP Master Plan will then be provided for final signature by the Crow Tribe's Chairman, Crow Tribal Water Rights Office Director, and Engineer of Record (Bartlett & West). The Master Plan is important as an overarching document with generalized approval of projects over the duration of the settlement with expected oversight of project specifications, funding adjustments, and other issues as they arise.

2. CIP Environmental Assessment

The CIP Environmental Assessment (EA) is also nearing completion. The CIP EA has been reviewed internally be Reclamation, and is scheduled to be distributed for a one month public comment period by September 15, 2014. Following the public comment period, a response to all comments will be prepared, and all EA documents are expected to be finalized. The issuance of a signed FONSI by Reclamation is anticipated by the end of 2014.

B. CIP Completed and Future Work

Construction work on the Crow Irrigation Project under the Settlement Act commenced in 2012, and has continued since that time but in a somewhat reduced scope of activities. Construction work on projects during this timeframe has been primarily limited to smaller rehabilitation projects, and is contingent upon final sign off on the CIP Master Plan to proceed forward at full scale construction. A number of large rehabilitation projects are scheduled to commence construction in calendar year 2015, and include major structures on the Bighorn and Forty Mile Units, as well as the Willow Creek Feeder Canal (Lodge Grass Feeder Canal).

Another significant issue that we have encountered (after engaging in more specific project reviews and implementation) is that the current condition of the irrigation structures and redesign options from original cost estimates by engineering consultants have increased in many cases (e.g., originally undersized bridges, culverts, etc.). This fact poses new challenges for the Tribe and Reclamation to fulfill the objectives of the CIP while staying within the $132 million budget. We recognize that this ultimately means that the Tribe will need to search for more creative solutions to resolve underlying unanticipated and major estimated design system flaws (based primarily on poor oversight and enforcement of the system by the BIA in the past).

One of the benefits of funding the rehabilitation and improvement of irrigation systems on Indian Reservations is that the results are tangible. You can see a tangible difference that Federal dollars make on the ground in the day-to-day functionality of the systems in Indian country. As such, we have provided a few examples below of what the CIP looked like before and after the Crow Water Settlement implantation began to demonstrate how the appropriated funds have made a difference on the Crow Reservation to rehabilitate and improve much needed segments of the CIP.

2012 Completed Projects

a. Agency Diversion

The Agency Diversion Riprap Repair project was completed by the Crow Tribe Water Rights Department (''CTWRD'') during the fall of 2012 and spring of 2013. Work completed under this project generally consisted of:

- Placing compacted soil to fill the eroded bank area on the east side of the Little Big Horn River.
- Placing geotextile fabric and rock to armor bank area.
- Site grading, surface restoration and seeding.

b. Lodge Grass No. 1

The Lodge Grass Canal No. 1 Headworks rehabilitation project was completed by the CTWRD during the winter of 2012 and 2013. Work completed under this project generally consisted of:

- Construction of cofferdams and dewatering in Lodge Grass Creek.
- Demolition of a portion of the old deteriorated headwall.
- Construction of a concrete overlay over the deteriorated headwall.
- Construction of two new concrete walkway support walls.
- Installation of a new steel walkway over Lodge Grass Creek.
- Site grading, surface restoration and seeding.

Before:    After:

c. Lodge Grass No. 2

The Lodge Grass Canal No. 2 Headworks rehabilitation project was completed by the CTWRD during the winter of 2012 and 2013. Work completed under this project generally consisted of:

- Construction of cofferdams and dewatering in Lodge Grass Creek.
- Demolition of a portion of the old headworks structure.
- Construction of new headwork structures including cast-in-place concrete walls and slab and installation of precast concrete box culverts and three slide gates.
- Construction of two new concrete walkway support walls.

- Installation of a new steel walkway over Lodge Grass Creek.
- Site grading, surface restoration and seeding.

Before:

After:

2. 2013 Completed Projects

a. Bighorn High Check Emergency Repair

Emergency repairs were completed in the spring of 2013 to stabilize the structure and to prevent its failure until it could be fully rehabilitated in FY 2015. Work consisted of the following:

- Backfill was imported to fill in the erosion
- Extended downstream concrete apron
- Install EPDM liner with riprap ballast to reduce further erosion

Before: After:

b. Reno O&M Road Improvements

It was determined that O&M road improvements were necessary from the Old Hwy 87 Frontage Road to the Reno Diversion Dam and Headworks. The improved road will provide all weather access to the Reno Diversion Dam and Headworks and Siphon. It will also help facilitate construction when the Reno Diversion Dam and Headworks and the Siphon are rehabilitated and for future O&M activities on the structures thereafter. The Reno Diversion Dam and Headworks is planned for rehabilitation in FY2015. The Reno Siphon is planned for replacement in FY2015.

Before:

After:

c. Rotten Grass Wasteway

It was determined that stabilization and erosion protection improvements were necessary for the Rotten Grass Wasteway. Immediate efforts were needed to protect the structure and downstream channel from further erosion and damage, and allow for continued operation of the wasteway.

Before:

After:

3. 2014 Completed Projects

a. High Check O&M Road Improvements

It was determined that O&M road improvements were necessary from the Little Owl Loop Road to the vicinity of High Check. The improved road would provide all weather access to High Check and the turnout for Lateral 728. It would also facilitate construction when High Check and High Drop are replaced and for future O&M activities on the structures thereafter.

Before: After:

4. Major Upcoming Construction Projects

There are a number of projects that are planned for 2015.

a. Willow Creek Feeder Canal Phase I, II, & III

- Install riprap below the diversion dam and headworks structures and install new slide gates on the headworks.
- Replace the existing stop logs in the wasteway with a slide gate and restore the radial gate to operation.
- Remove brush and trees and reshape the canal prism.
- Install earthen lining for select reaches of the canal to address seepage concerns.
- Construction of a new terminal drop structure.

b. Reno Diversion Dam, Headworks, and Flume

- Install one Obermeyer gate and construct a radial gate sluiceway.
- Remove and construct a new headwork structure.
- Remove and replace existing ramp flume.

c. Forty Mile Headworks & O&M Road

- Remove the existing headworks and construct a new structure with a new slide gate.
- Remove the existing Parshall flume and constructing a new Parshall flume.
- Stabilize river bank adjacent to the new structure.
- Complete improvements to the existing O&M road including leveling, grading, and placing gravel.

d. Bighorn High Check

- Removing old structure and replacing with a new check structure.

V. Conclusion

Every Indian irrigation system is unique and poses its own challenges. In our case, we are dealing with several decades of deferred maintenance on the CIP that must be remedied on a strategic and forward-thinking approach in order to make the most out of the Crow Water Settlement funds. As we make progress, we will also have to ensure that the future funds for operation, maintenance and replacement are collected from users on a timely basis or we will face the same funding shortfalls that plagued the system in the past. Even though we have experienced a few temporary setbacks in the implementation of the Settlement, we are headed in the right direction and are optimistic that the CIP will ultimately be restored to the state it was originally intended to be for the Crow Indian Reservation.

The CHAIRMAN. You are getting pretty darned good at this, Mr. Chairman. You have two seconds left. Thank you very much for your testimony.

Governor Paisano, you are up.

STATEMENT OF HON. STUART PAISANO, GOVERNOR, PUEBLO OF SANDIA

Mr. PAISANO. Good afternoon, and greetings from the Pueblo of Sandia. Chairman Tester, Vice Chairman Barrasso, and our good friend and Senator Tom Udall and Committee members, thank you for the opportunity to appear before you today and to testify concerning some of the problems with the irrigation infrastructure serving the Six Middle Rio Grande Pueblos in New Mexico.

The Coalition of the Six Middle Rio Grande Pueblos, as the name implies, is comprised of the six Pueblos whose lands are within the Middle Rio Grande Valley: the Pueblos of Cochiti, Santo Domingo, San Felipe, Santa Ana, Sandia and Isleta. The Coalition, which used to be called the Pueblo Irrigation Committee, focuses exclusively on water and irrigation issues.

The six Pueblos are the aboriginal occupants of the valley, which now includes close to a million people located primarily in and around the City of Albuquerque. The Pueblos' lands are largely rural in character and we continue to practice and rely on irrigated agriculture for our culture, as we have for centuries.

Unfortunately, the six Pueblos, largely because they are located in the most populous area of the State, no longer have their own separate diversions and canals. Instead, the Pueblos now depend on irrigation facilities that are owned by the U.S. Bureau of Reclamation, but which are operated and maintained by an entity known as the Middle Rio Grande Conservancy District, or the MRGCD. Under Federal law the MRGCD is obligated to maintain certain on-Pueblo irrigation facilities and to deliver water to meet congressionally and federally recognized prior and paramount water rights of the Pueblos, without charge, in exchange for vital rights-of-way across the Pueblos.

For congressionally-recognized water rights for the Pueblos' newly reclaimed lands served by the same Middle Rio Grande Project, the Bureau of Indian Affairs contracts with the MRGCD for operation and maintenance services. It is a complicated agreement and one that, frankly, has historically not worked for the Pueblos. Specifically, irrigation facilities that only serve Pueblo lands have not been maintained as well as those serving non-Pueblo lands. Consequently, the Pueblos often have a more difficult time than our non-Indian neighbors irrigating their lands and obtaining operations and maintenance services. Attached to my statement are some pictures illustrating the MRGCD's unequal maintenance of facilities on the Pueblo versus non-Pueblo lands.

The irrigation facilities serving the Coalition Pueblos were not reviewed and evaluated by the GAO back in 2006 because they are not part of a BIA project, but it certainly would have been useful had the GAO done such a review.

The BIA must do a better job in ensuring that the MRGCD operates and maintains facilities serving the Pueblo lands on an equal basis with facilities serving non-Pueblo lands. To its credit, the BIA has recently shown an interest in achieving this goal and Director Black has become personally involved in negotiating for a new O&M agreement between the BIA and the MRGCD. I also understand that Director Black and Assistant Secretary Washburn have worked to secure sufficient funds for a conditions assessment of irrigation facilities on Pueblo lands and that BIA expects to enter into a contract for this assessment work next month.

While the Coalition Pueblos greatly appreciate Assistant Secretary Washburn's and Director Black's efforts, serious problems still remain. Each year the vast majority of the limited funds budgeted by BIA for operations, maintenance and betterment of irrigation facilities serving the six Pueblos goes for water delivery operations and routine maintenance, such as mowing and dredging, not betterment work. Thus, our antiquated and inefficient irrigation systems continue to deteriorate. Without improved and efficient irrigation systems, there is little incentive for our farmers to invest in higher value crops or to increase the acreage they irrigate.

Inefficient systems also means that more water must be diverted from the Rio Grande, which is a river that is sufficiently over-appropriated. These problems were recognized several years ago by former Senators Domenici and Bingaman who co-sponsored legislation passed in 2009 known as the Rio Grande Pueblos Irrigation Infrastructure Improvement Act. It directs the Secretary, through the Bureau of Reclamation, to conduct a study of irrigation infrastructure serving all of the Pueblos in the Rio Grande Valley, based on the results of that study, to develop a list of projects to repair, rehabilitate or reconstruct irrigation infrastructure. The Act further authorizes an appropriation of $4 million for the study, and $60 million over a ten-year period for irrigation system repairs and projects to modernize our systems and to make them more efficient.

Unfortunately, funds have yet to be appropriated for any of the work directed by the Act. To address this, Senators Udall and Heinrich recently introduced a drought relief bill, S. 2470, which includes as one of its provisions reauthorization of the Pueblos Irrigation Infrastructure Improvement Act. This reauthorization would extend the time period for, and increase the amount of, funding under the Act. The Coalition Pueblos strongly support the reauthorization and the appropriations to accomplish the Act's purpose.

Thank you again for inviting me to testify this afternoon and I will be pleased to respond to any questions.

[The prepared statement of Mr. Paisano follows:]

PREPARED STATEMENT OF HON. STUART PAISANO, GOVERNOR, PUEBLO OF SANDIA

Chairman Tester, Vice Chairman Barrasso and Committee members, thank you for the opportunity to appear before you today and to testify concerning some of the problems with the irrigation infrastructure serving the Six Middle Rio Grande Pueblos in New Mexico.

The Coalition of Six Middle Rio Grande Pueblos, as the name implies, is comprised of the six Pueblo tribes whose lands are within the Middle Rio Grande Valley—the Pueblos of Cochiti, Santo Domingo, San Felipe, Santa Ana, Sandia and Isleta. The Coalition, which used to be called the Pueblo Irrigation Committee, focuses exclusively on water and irrigation issues.

The six Pueblos are the aboriginal occupants of the Valley, which now includes close to a million people located primarily in and around the City of Albuquerque. Unlike Albuquerque and its environs, however, the Pueblos' lands are still largely rural in character and we continue to practice and rely on irrigated agriculture, as we have for centuries. And—unlike relatively newer irrigation projects serving lands that were never historically irrigated—the Pueblos' agriculture, and the diversions, ditches and water associated with it, have long been an integral part of Pueblos' culture and traditions.

Unfortunately, the six Pueblos, largely because they are located in the most populous area of the state and surrounded by non-Indian lands, no longer have their own separate diversions and canals. Instead, the Pueblos now depend on irrigation facilities that are owned by the U.S. Bureau of Reclamation, [1] but which are operated and maintained by an entity known as the Middle Rio Grande Conservancy District or the MRGCD. Under federal law the MRGCD is obligated to maintain certain on-Pueblo irrigation facilities and to deliver water to meet Congressionally-recognized prior and paramount water rights of the Pueblos, without charge, in exchange for vital rights-of-way across the Pueblos. For Congressionally-recognized water rights for Pueblo "newly reclaimed lands" served by the same Middle Rio Grande Project, the Bureau of Indian Affairs contracts with the MRGCD for operation and maintenance services. It is a complicated arrangement and one that, frankly, has historically not worked well for the six Pueblos.

Specifically, irrigation facilities that only serve Pueblo lands have not been maintained as well as those serving non-Pueblo lands. Consequently, the Pueblos often have a more difficult time than our non-Indian neighbors irrigating their lands and obtaining operations and maintenance services. Attached to my statement are some pictures illustrating the MRGCD's unequal maintenance of facilities on Pueblo versus non-Pueblo lands. The irrigation facilities serving the Coalition Pueblos were presumably not reviewed and evaluated by the GAO back in 2006 because they are not part of a BIA project, but it certainly would have been useful had GAO done such a review.

The BIA must do a better job in ensuring that the MRGCD operates and maintains facilities serving Pueblo lands on an equal basis with facilities serving non-Pueblo lands. To its credit, the BIA has recently shown an interest in achieving this goal and Director Black has even become personally involved in negotiations for a new O & M agreement between the BIA and the MRGCD. I also understand that Director Black and Assistant Secretary Washburn have worked to secure sufficient funds for a conditions assessment of irrigation facilities on Pueblo lands and that BIA expects to enter into a contract for this assessment work next month.

While the Coalition Pueblos greatly appreciate Assistant Secretary Washburn's and Director Black's efforts, serious problems remain. Each year the vast majority of the limited funds budgeted by BIA for operations, maintenance and betterment of irrigation facilities serving the six Pueblos goes for water-delivery operations and routine maintenance, such as mowing and dredging, not betterment work. Thus, our antiquated and inefficient irrigation systems continue to deteriorate. Without improved and efficient irrigation systems, there is little incentive for our farmers to invest in higher value crops or to increase the acreage they irrigate. Inefficient systems also mean more water must be diverted from the Rio Grande—a river that is significantly over-appropriated.

These problems were recognized several years ago by former Senators Domenici and Bingaman who co-sponsored legislation passed in 2009, known as the Rio Grande Pueblos Irrigation Infrastructure Improvement Act. This Act was drafted primarily by Mike Connor, the current Deputy Secretary of the Interior and former Commissioner of the Bureau of Reclamation. It directs the Secretary, through the Bureau of Reclamation, to conduct a study of irrigation infrastructure serving all of the Rio Grande Pueblos and, based on the results of that study, to develop a list of projects to repair, rehabilitate or reconstruct irrigation infrastructure. The Act further authorizes an appropriation of $4 million for the study, and $60 million over a ten year period for irrigation system repairs and projects to modernize our systems and make them more efficient.

Unfortunately, funds have yet to be appropriated for any of the work directed by the Act. To address this, Senators Udall and Heinrich recently introduced a drought relief bill, S. 2470, which includes as one of its provisions reauthorization of the Pueblo Irrigation Infrastructure Improvement Act. This reauthorization would extend the time period for, and increase the amount of, the funding under the Act. The Coalition Pueblos strongly support this reauthorization and the requisite appropriations to accomplish the Act's purposes.

Thank you again for inviting me to testify this afternoon and I will be pleased to respond to any questions.

Attachments

---

[1] Except for the Isleta diversion dam, which is owned by the Pueblo of Isleta and is currently operated by the MRGCD without any legal authorization.

Sinkhole on ditch bank. Causes leaking and safety concerns for vehicles on ditch road.

Damaged MRGCD culvert under Pueblo road.

Corrales Feeder on Sandia Pueblo, October 8, 2013

Corrales Feeder in Corrales, October 8, 2013

Albuquerque Main at north Sandia Reservation Boundary. Clean ditch bank in background is in Bernalillo. Vegetation in foreground is on Sandia Pueblo, October 8, 2013

Albuquerque Main at north Sandia Reservation Boundary, picture taken from the Bernalillo side looking toward Sandia Pueblo. Clean ditch bank in foreground is in Bernalillo. Vegetation in background is on Sandia Pueblo, October 8, 2013

Sandia Acequia on Sandia Pueblo, October 8, 2013

Sandia Acequia in Bernalillo, October 8, 2013

Ranchitos Drain at Santa Ana Pueblo South Boundary – Looking North toward Santa Ana Pueblo, October 2013

Ranchitos Drain South of Santa Ana Pueblo in Bernalillo, October 2013

Albuquerque Main Canal at Santa Ana Pueblo South Boundary – Looking North to Santa Ana,
October 2013

Albuquerque Main Canal at Santa Ana Pueblo South Boundary – Looking South to Bernalillo,
October 2013

Albuquerque Main Canal at Santa Ana Pueblo South Boundary -- Looking South to Bernalillo
(Access Gate on Left marks Santa Ana Pueblo South Boundary), October 2013

Honorable Chairman Jon Tester and Honorable Members of the Committee, thank you for leaving the hearing record open for additional written testimony to the Senate Committee on Indian Affairs Oversight Hearings on Irrigation Projects in Indian Country. We respectfully submit the following for the record.

The Pueblo of Sandia has been engaged in developing its water and related infrastructure to provide for our people, protect the land and strengthen our self-governance. As Governor Paisano testified before the Committee on September 10, 2014; water is vital to our culture, religion, livelihood and economic security. Here we would like to provide a bit of background on the Pueblo of Sandia's efforts do what the federal government has fallen short in doing under its "trust responsibility". We would also request support for a project which has ties to irrigation and habitat that we will describe later in this written submittal. We have understood for a few decades now that the trust responsibility is not just the responsibility of the Bureau of Indian Affairs but resides with other Departments and agencies of the federal government as well. The list of Federal Departments and Agencies that we interact with is almost as extensive as the whole of Federal government itself.

Science and technology is now telling us what those that have gone before us have known for centuries, all water on our Mother Earth is connected in some form be it snow, rain, surface or ground water. To afford our People the life and livelihood from our remaining lands; we have developed our potable water supplies, wastewater treatment facilities that incorporated reuse of water, we have developed drainage structures to capture run off as well as protect life and facilities and we have developed rain catchments to help the wildlife survive in times of drought. We are also undertaking through the P.L. 93-638 process irrigation infrastructure improvements within our lands. In 1993 we attained Treatment as a State and took primacy for the Pueblo's water quality standards as approved by the US Environmental Protection Agency and have used our standards to improve water quality not only on our lands but beyond our trust lands as well. We hope one day to allow our people to safely draw water from the Mother River (the Rio Grande) with earthen pots and renew Centuries old practices.

This work is never done nor will it ever be. Water related facilities will continue to be needed, existing infrastructure and facilities will need to be operated and maintained and all of this will be part of our capital planning process that will include high standards for the development, operations, maintenance and replacement on our lands. This work must continue despite the continued hurdles found in the lack of federal and state funding, bureaucratic systems and regulations that delay development and increase the costs of development. As noted by Principal Deputy Assistant Secretary, Lawrence Roberts before this Committee on September 10, 2014; "it is a daunting challenge similar to other infrastructure challenges faced across the Nation". For our small Sandia Pueblo nation of people it is indeed a daunting task; a task that we take one step at a time knowing the full scope of the task will continue with new generations.

Now to the specific request for support that is chosen as it could serve as an example of pooling resources in a cooperative effort of federal, state and Pueblo people. Attached is a white paper on the Corrales Siphon which is being exposed to risks of failure due to the incising of the Rio Grande.*The incising is believed to be the result of lack of sedimentation due to the Cochiti Dam, a facility of the US Army Corps of Engineers. The Corrales Siphon was built about 1933 and is part of the federal works turned over to the Middle Rio Grande Conservancy District. Unfortunately the MRGCD is already drawing on its cash reserves for current operations and likely will not have the resources to fully underwrite the Corrales Siphon project that must include consideration for the habitat and ground water levels that surround the Siphon. It should be known that the Corrales Siphon is a vital economic link that crosses the Middle Rio Grande.

What we ask is that our stretch of the Mother River not be forgotten in the massive projects and billions in funding that this Nation needs for rebuilding its deteriorating infrastructure. What we request is that you as Honorable Committee Members ask each Federal Department, Agency and New Mexico State agency representative that may appear before you if they are willing to assist the Pueblo of Sandia in taking each step to address what is indeed a daunting task.

Thank you very much for your kind attention to the Pueblo of Sandia's contributions to what is indeed a National challenge.

---

* The information referred to has been retained in the Committee files.

The CHAIRMAN. Thank you, Governor. Thank you for your testimony.

Council Member Ruth Jim, you may proceed.

STATEMENT OF HON. RUTH JIM, COUNCIL MEMBER, CONFEDERATED TRIBES AND BANDS OF THE YAKAMA NATION

Ms. JIM. [Greeting in native tongue.]

Good afternoon. My name is Ruth Jim. I would like to recognize the Creator, because water is very sacred. Without water, irrigation can't happen.

Thank you for allowing me to testify today. I will now summarize my testimony. I am a member of the Yakama Nation's Tribal Council and Chair of the Tribal Council's Roads, Irrigation and Land Committee. Our Tribal Council is the governing body of the Yakama Nation and of the Yakama Reservation.

I am testifying today because the Bureau of Indian Affairs, through the Wapato Irrigation Project, WIP, needs to satisfy its trust duty to the Yakama Nation and its members. WIP has had some serious problems, and it is falling apart. There have been numerous studies of the WIP by the GAO and the Department of Interior. The BIA knows what the problems are. The BIA needs to fix WIP so WIP can deliver water to our Indian lands.

The problems can be solved if the BIA spends the money needed to fix WIP, so that it can deliver water reserved in our treaty of 1855 to our lands. Old structures need to be replaced or repaired. WIP is 100 years old this year, and needs work. The problem is especially hard for our Indian lands. Most of the lands within WIP are owned by the Yakama Nation and its members. Many of our Indian lands cannot get water from WIP because the project cannot physically deliver water to all of the land within the project boundaries. In some cases, it would require new canals, or in other cases, the lands, for instance, on steeply-sloped areas, wouldn't hold water.

However, WIP still continues to bill us for O&M, even when water isn't delivered. Many of our lands are also not being irrigated because the BIA has not helped us get the lands developed. The BIA has both failed to help Indian farmers develop the lands and failed to get the land leased by others if the Indian owner wants to lease the land. Many of our lands are also in probate and are fractionated, which makes management of them difficult. In some cases, especially when highly fractionated, we do not even know all of the owners. The lands that are not in production are referred to as idle lands.

Prior to 1980, the BIA helped fund the WIP operating budget. Suddenly, the BIA designated WIP as a Class 1 self-sustaining project, even though it had never been self-sustaining. The combination of having 20 percent or more of the project lands in idle status, the loss of BIA funds and the sugar beet industry leaving the area all occurred in close proximity to one another and created a serious financial burden on WIP. While the BIA had already totally shirked its responsibility to repair the project, it then got worse and deferred maintenance became standard operating procedure.

There are solutions to these problems and we are working on them. There are identified lands we hope to move to production. There are areas outside of WIP, but on the reservation on which we are examining the potential of transferring WIP water rights. We are trying to be innovative, but we cannot solve these problems without more time and an influx of Federal funds. The Congress should direct that the Class I self-sustaining status be changed to its former status.

We also ask that Congress please enact S. 715, including the Barrasso amendment, which is now Title IV of that bill, as reported by the Energy and Natural Resources Committee. Title IV will quite appropriately allow projects such as WIP to access the Reclamation Fund. Washington State is a Reclamation Act State and that statute creating this fund indicates that it is ''to be used in the examination and survey for and the construction and maintenance of irrigation works for the storage, diversion and development of waters for the reclamation of arid and semi-arid lands in the said States.''

There is no reason why irrigation projects on Indian reservations such as WIP or Wind River in Wyoming should be denied access to the Reclamation Fund dollars, particularly at a time when the fund is flush and we understand they have $12 billion in it. These funds would definitely allow us to fix the project and use our treaty water on our reservation.

Once again, I thank you, and I would be pleased to answer any questions. I also have an article from the Yakama Herald where

the BIA was almost, the water irrigators filed suit against the BIA, a tort claim, to submit with my testimony. Thank you.
[The prepared statement of Ms. Jim follows:]

PREPARED STATEMENT OF HON. RUTH JIM, COUNCIL MEMBER, CONFEDERATED TRIBES AND BANDS OF THE YAKAMA NATION

My name is Ruth Jim. I am a member of the Yakama Nation's Tribal Council and Chair of the Tribal Council's Roads, Irrigation and Land Committee. Our Tribal Council is the governing body of the Yakama Nation and of the Yakama Reservation. For many years our Tribe has been dealing with problems related to the Wapato Irrigation Project, a Bureau of Indian Affairs irrigation project on the Yakama Reservation.

I. Background

The Wapato Irrigation Project ("WIP" or "Project"), operated by the Bureau of Indian Affairs (BIA), is an Indian irrigation project located entirely on the Yakama Indian Reservation. WIP operates under the direction of the Bureau of Indian Affairs Regional Director. The Yakama Reservation covers an area of approximately 1.7 million acres in south central Washington State. Water was reserved by the Yakama Nation in the Treaty of June 9, 1855. The Nation's Treaty water is delivered through WIP to Tribal and allotted lands. The three units comprising the WIP have a combined total between 140,000 and 150,000 acres of land within their boundaries.

Irrigation under the auspices of the BIA began in the Nineteenth Century on the Reservation in the Toppenish Creek area shortly after the Reservation was created. Irrigation also occurred from Ahtanum Creek which forms the northern border of the Reservation. Assistance by the Federal Government for the provision of irrigation water from the Yakima River itself was initiated by the Indian Service (which is now the BIA) with the construction of the Irwin or Old Reservation Canal in 1896–1897.

WIP was authorized by the United States government and planned by the BIA in the early 1900s. In 1912, a report from the Department of the Interior was presented to Congress which confirmed that the water provided to the Yakama Nation from the Yakima River was inadequate. As a result of this report the Secretary was ordered in the 1912 Congressional appropriations act to develop a plan to get more Treaty water onto the Reservation:

> That the Secretary of the Interior be, and he is hereby, authorized and directed to investigate the conditions on the Yakama Indian Reservation . . . with a view to determine the best, most practicable and most feasible plan for providing water for such lands . . .

Act of August 24, 1912, 37 Stat. 518

A report was also produced by Congress that recommended that work proceed on enlargement of WIP for the use of additional Treaty water for the Yakama Reservation. "Report of the Condition of the Yakama Indian Reservation, Washington," H. Rept. Doc. No. 1299 (62nd Cong., 3d Sess.) (Jan. 24, 1913). Pursuant to this authority and this Report, Congress appointed a commission to investigate and make recommendations on providing additional Treaty irrigation water for the Yakama Nation and its Reservation and the "construction of an irrigation system" on it. Act of June 30, 1913, 38 Stat. 77, Sec. 23. Most of the facilities comprising the Project were constructed between 1917 and 1950.

WIP is divided into three units. The surface water for the bulk of the irrigated land is diverted to the Wapato-Satus Unit from the Yakima River near Parker Washington. There are also smaller irrigation units on Ahtanum Creek and on Toppenish and Simcoe Creeks which deliver natural flow from those creeks for irrigation. Of the designated lands entitled to delivery of water through the Wapato-Satus Unit of WIP, a disproportionate number, about 27, 973 acres are idle Indian lands as of 2000. "Idle" means in this context that these lands are entitled to a delivery of water through WIP but are not being irrigated. The land is not being irrigated due to a number of factors outside of the control of the owner including an inability of WIP to actually deliver water to many of those acres. Some of the idle land included in the project is marginal for irrigation due to slopes and other factors such as its location near the end of laterals resulting in poor water supply. Such land can be farmed but requires the investment of a great deal of money that is not available. Up to 7,000 acres of such land was included in the project in the 1930's with the understanding that it would not pay O & M because it could only occasionally be farmed. The problems for these lands specifically and the Project in general can be corrected but it will take a great deal of time and money to do so.

II. Problems With the Wapato Irrigation Project

As the above shows, WIP has been in existence for over a hundred years. Many of the constructed works are between 50 and 100 years old. Because of a lack of funds, necessary maintenance for this Project has been repeatedly postponed. As it relates to all of the BIA irrigation projects the Government Accountability Office has concluded that because " . . . .the BIA has historically not had adequate funds to operate and maintain the projects, the projects are in a serious state of disrepair." *Indian Irrigation Projects—Numerous Issues Need to Be Addressed to Improve Project Management and Financial Sustainability* GAO 06–314 (Feb. 2006) at p. 30. Reviews of WIP, in particular, have repeatedly found problems in funding. In 1995 the Inspector General's office of the BIA found that " . . . sufficient funds were not available to properly maintain the Project, and it has deteriorated to the extent that several studies have concluded that the continued ability of the Project to deliver water is in doubt." *Final Audit Report of the Wapato Irrigation Project, Bureau of Indian Affairs,* (No. 95–I–1402) (Sept. 30, 1995) at p. 5. The Inspector General found that WIP budgets would exclude the "costs of needed capital improvements . . . " thus creating a situation where " . . . maintenance was performed only on an exceptional basis, whenever funds were available to the Project." *Id.* at p. 6. The Inspector General concluded that " . . . [t]he lack of adequate maintenance, combined with the increased age of Project facilities, has resulted in the deterioration of the Project." *Id.* This was followed by a later GAO report on WIP. *See, Indian Programs, BIA's Management of the Wapato Irrigation Project,* GAO/RCED–97–124 (May 1997). Most recently the BIA has released a report prepared for it by Dowl HKM which estimated that the cost of rehabilitation and replacement of failing WIP facilities to be between 136 and 276 million dollars in 2013 dollars. *See, Engineering Evaluation and Condition Assessment, Wapato Irrigation Project, Vol. 1* (Oct. 2013) at p. vi (Executive Summary).

Part of the problem is due to the age of the Project. However, this problem was exacerbated by the Department of Interior's decision in the early 1980's to classify the Wapato-Satus Unit as "financially able to pay the full cost." *Report of the Current Status of Indian Irrigation Projects Administered by the Bureau of Indian Affairs* (May 1988) at p. 23, 25. The Wapato-Satus Unit was arbitrarily listed as a Category I project which the BIA called one that is " . . . self-supporting, and water users are required to pay the full cost of operation." *Id.* at p. 23. But WIP was never self-supporting. Hundreds if not thousands of acres of Indian land within the Wapato-Satus Unit have never been irrigated resulting in less land producing adequate funds to pay O & M.[1]

Until the 1980s, appropriated funds subsidized the operation and maintenance costs for this idle land. The cessation of annual appropriated funds in the 1980s unfortunately coincided with the increase of idle lands. Marginal lands had previously been planted with sugar beets. When the sugar beet industry collapsed in the Yakama area about the same time, the idle lands increased dramatically. The U.S. should have determined then that WIP was no longer self-supporting (without conceding it ever was) and started providing appropriated funds but failed to do so. This meant that there were fewer funds from O & M coming into WIP to pay for its operation precisely at the same time that federal appropriations also stopped.[2]

While there has been disagreement with BIA concerning the causes of the deferred maintenance problem on WIP and the liability of Indian owners of idle land to pay the O & M, there is no disagreement about the underlying deferred maintenance problem. Indian people and the Yakama Nation itself have been unwilling to pay O & M on this long term idle land (including land that has never been irrigated) merely to subsidize the federal government and non-Indian farmers. In many cases WIP cannot even deliver water to these idle lands due to deteriorated or nonexistent delivery infrastructure.

The deferred maintenance has helped cause the following problems among others:

---

[1] Indeed some Tribal and individual lands that were designated for the delivery of WIP water were known to be marginal lands at the time they were included and have rarely or never been irrigated.

[2] The fact that the BIA would charge Indian land owners O & M fees for water delivery on lands that had never received any water was confounding to the Indian land owners. Since the land (a) wasn't getting any water; and (b) wasn't generating any income from crops to pay O & M, many of the land owners didn't or couldn't pay their assessments and there were no longer federal funds to help make up the difference.

a.) Supplies of water delivered through WIP are increasingly unreliable due to deteriorating infrastructure. Last year there was a failure of pumps on Unit 2 which caused a delay and failure to deliver water to certain trust and fee lands serviced by the Unit 2 Canal of WIP. Many other key facilities critical to the operation of WIP are in a similar state of disrepair. For example, the Main Diversion headgates and flow control system are failing making it difficult to open and close the gates and regulate diversions from the Yakima River.

b.) Leaky, unlined delivery canals have made irrigation deliveries more difficult and inefficient. Lack of annual cleaning and maintenance programs for these canals exacerbate these problems.

c.) An increasing inability to convey irrigation water within the WIP delivery system has made it more difficult to fully deliver water to idle designated trust and allottee lands. This has led to parcels designated for delivery not being leased and a loss of assessed income to the WIP.

d.) Antiquated diversion structures and leaky, unlined delivery canals result in poor water management and conveyance losses. This has required the diversion of more water to meet irrigation requirements on Ahtanum, Toppenish and Simcoe Creeks. Downstream from the diversion points the project spills canal water and discharges polluted return flows to Toppenish and Simcoe Creek, then diverts these return flows onto other portions of the WIP Project thus often impairing other natural resources in these Creeks and degrading Cultural sites. While instream flow for fish and other aquatic life is senior in priority to all irrigation rights, pressure to divert extra water for irrigation inevitably puts pressure on the environment and the Yakama Nation's natural and cultural resources. The Wapato Irrigation Project has a profound impact on Toppenish Creek and its tributary Simcoe Creek, which harbor their own distinct population of steelhead trout. Ahtanum, Toppenish and Simcoe creeks are used as both a water supply and a waste conduit by the Project. The Yakama Nation has conceptual designs for using natural stream water more efficiently, and for rerouting Project spills and return flows directly to canals for use on Project lands without entering these natural streams, but the Project lacks the funding to fully develop and implement them.

III. Conclusion

The chronic deferred maintenance can be reduced if Congress does the following:

a.) Adopts S. 715, particularly Title IV, so as to allow access to the Reclamation Fund (which now has over $11 billion dollars in it) to be used to address deferred maintenance on Indian Irrigation Projects and to identify WIP as a priority project for the use of these funds.

b.) Amend the Yakima River Basin Water Enhancement Project (YRBWEP), P.L. 103–434, to increase funding levels for proposed WIP improvements to account for inflation and projected increased project costs. YRBWEP currently provides $23 million in authorization for WIP improvements. YRBWEP was enacted to address some of the water availability and fisheries issues both on and off Reservation. Unfortunately, this authorizing language for the Yakama Reservation, which was passed during the 103rd Congress, does not provide for adjustments to current day dollars. This lack of adjustment to current day dollars is inconsistent with other sections of YRBWEP which do provide adjustments for inflation for other portions of the Act. We believe that this exclusion of the WIP improvement project funding from having an inflation adjustment was a technical oversight. This is an important issue to resolve because funding of the *Priority Irrigation Water Conservation and Management Measures Plan for the Wapato Irrigation Project* (Priority Measures Plan)[3] developed through the YRBWEP program will require approximately $53 million (in 2004 dollars) to complete. The Priority Measures Plan was developed to identify priority items for WIP conservation and improvements after a much more comprehensive list of re-

---

[3] The Plan was partially certified by the Secretary of Interior for funding and implementation through the YRBWEP. Its major components consisted of upgrading the Satus Unit of the WIP through installation of a new downriver pumped diversion on the Yakima River and piping water to users in the Satus, improved measurement facilities to enable better Project water management and measurement of on-farm water deliveries, development of a tiered O&M assessment classification for irrigated parcels and creation of a water transfer/leasing system to enable irrigation water transfer within the WIP.

habilitation and reconstruction items for WIP were determined to exceed the YRBWEP authorization. Thus a shorter (although certainly not complete) list of priority items was identified. Without the ability to adjust the original $23 million authorized for this project for inflation and provide an increase in the original authorization limit amount, YRBWEP will not provide the necessary funding to complete the construction of the conservation measures outlined in the WIP Priority Measures Plan.

c.) Congress should also request that the Secretary of the Interior consult concerning the YRBWEP Priority Measures Plan and help implement this so as to address the underlying WIP problems. The Priority Measures Plan was partially certified on August 28, 2006 in a letter from the Secretary's office. However, the Secretary did not at that time certify two components of the Plan concerning a change in the WIP operation and maintenance rate structure and a plan to facilitate water leasing and transfer within the Reservation. The Secretary has agreed to continue to work on this without certification to address the WIP structural problems. We ask your help in facilitating resolution of these issues and provide authorized funding for these key components of the Wapato Irrigation Project.

Attachment

WATER WORRIES PERSIST WITH WAPATO IRRIGATION PROJECT—POSTED ON JULY 2, 2014—BY ROSS COURTNEY, YAKIMA HERALD-REPUBLIC

WHITE SWAN—Federal authorities have declined to award damages to farmers who claimed they lost crops last year due to neglience that contributed to broken pumps and motors at the beleaguered Wapato Irrigation Project.

Now many of those growers plan to sue.

"They denied every one of those claims," cattle rancher Larry Doman said. "Paid nothing, accepted nc responsibility."

After a few months of easing tensions this spring, frustration is high again on the Unit 2 canal, a remote ditch that irrigates 3,336 acres of orchards, hay, mint and other crops southeast of White Swan, along the base of the Toppenish Ridge.

Officials with the Bureau of Indian Affairs, which operates the Wapato Irrigation Project, denied a total of between $750,000 and $1 million in tort claims filed by ii farmers who say a June 2013 failure at the pumphouse that supplies the canal left them with inadequate water during the hottest stretch of summer.

Fields of corn and hay withered and died as growers prioritized their irrigation rotation on the highest value crops.

Bureau attorneys argued the farmers provided no evidence the problems were created by negligence.

"After reviewing your claim, I find no credible evidence to establish any negligent or wrongful act or omission on the part of the government in this matter that would qualify for compensation under the FTCA (Federal Tort Claims Act)," wrote Alexandra James, the regional solicitor for the bureau in Portland, in a letter to all ii growers. "Accordingly, your claim is hereby denied."

Some of the growers are searching for attorneys to help them take the fight to federal court.

"I can't blame them," said Bodie Shaw, deputy regional director of the bureau's Northwest Regional Office in Portland. "I've been a farmer. If put in the same situation, I would do the same thing."

Doman is trying to rally support for a class-action case, hoping to find strength in numbers.

"The smart move for these guys is for all of us to band together," Doman said.

Some farmers are preparing an appeal directly to the BIA while also exploring a lawsuit, which must be filed within six months, said Aaron Olson, another denied Unit 2 rancher.

Troubles with equipment and canals are nothing new on the 17 irrigation districts operated by the bureau throughout the West. Scathing Government Accountability Office reports dating back to the 1970s decry weed-choked canals, dilapidated fish screens and numerous other maintenance deficiencies, as well as hundreds of millions of dollars in funding shortages due to complicated assessments and billing disputes.

The irrigation projects must pay for their own maintenance and operations expenses through grower assessments. They receive no subsidies from the federal government, Shaw said.

The Wapato Irrigation Project, which supplies Yakima River irrigation water to 225 square miles of the Yakama reservation, is the largest of the 17 and it has the same problems as the rest. But things were worse than usual last year on the Unit 2 canal.

The canal is supplied by the Toppenish Creek Pumphouse, built in 1933 and housed with World War II-era equipment.

Early last summer, a pipe that burst drenched pumps and motors, forcing officials to haul in temporary pumps, which ended up having their own mechanical glitches.

The problems combined to leave growers with rationed water during the hottest periods of the summer and prompted the project to send all three motors and some of the pumps to Portland, Idaho and Spokane for repairs to the tune of nearly $650,000.

''They're arguing that no WIP employee is responsible for those pumps going down,'' Olson, using an expletive, said. He lost much of his corn and hay last year.

Both farmers and irrigation project officials have discussed the need for maintenance, specifically at the Toppenish Creek Pumphouse, at least as early as 2011, according to meeting minutes and letters of the Yakama Reservation Irrigation District, the association of water clients that pays the Wapato Irrigation Project through annual assessments.

''We were screaming this needed to be taken care of,'' Olson said.

Meanwhile, the pumphouse problems still are not completely fixed.

The facility has a total of four pumps.

One is a small ''primer'' pump, used just in the startup process each season.

The biggest is a 1,500-horsepower machine that, when operating properly, sends roughly 60 cubic feet of water from a Toppenish Creek pool up the slope of Toppenish Ridge to the headwaters of the Unit 2 canal.

Two others are 800-horsepower backup pumps that together provide about the same amount.

Earlier this spring, the two smaller pumps were reinstalled and hooked up to their motors. They are now providing 57 cubic feet of water—just shy of the canal's capacity of 60.

The motor of the big pump, sent away for rebuilding, still is not working. Meanwhile, one of the smaller pumps has a bearing with a tendency to get too hot, said Ed Lewis, administrator of the Wapato Irrigation Project.

That means the whole operation is relying on dicey backup equipment, much like driving a car aroum on an already bald spare tire, the growers argue.

Lewis said Riverside Electric Motor & Pump Specialists, the Parma, Idaho, contractor hired to rebuik the motor for the large pump, delivered by the May 31 deadline. But electrical problems have plagued the equipment since then and the contractor's electrician took weeks to visit the Yakima Valley to diagnose it himself, Lewis said.

Now, the equipment is scheduled to be repaired by July 7, Lewis said.

The contractor has reliably repaired equipment before, Lewis said. But he admitted he is getting frustrated.

''If we can't get this thing resolved ... we'll have to start talking about voiding out the contract, doing something there,'' he said.

Simply buying new pumps is way out of the project's price range, Lewis said. They would have to be custom-built.

Lewis declined to discuss the tort claims but disagreed that neglect caused the problems.

''I would disagree with that statement,'' he said.

The CHAIRMAN. Thank you, Councilwoman Jim. I appreciate your testimony.

Mitchel Cottenoir, you are up.

STATEMENT OF MITCHEL T. COTTENOIR, TRIBAL WATER ENGINEER, EASTERN SHOSHONE AND NORTHERN ARAPAHO TRIBES OFFICE OF THE TRIBAL WATER ENGINEER

Mr. COTTENOIR. Chairman Tester, Vice Chairman Barrasso and members of the Committee, thank you for inviting me to represent the Eastern Shoshone and Northern Arapaho Tribes to appear before you today.

I have submitted a detailed statement and now I will summarize that statement. As Senator Barrasso earlier stated, little has changed on the Wind River Irrigation Project since the April 2011 field hearing held in Riverton, Wyoming. Operation and maintenance assessments have continued to rise and deferred maintenance continues to rise as well. The Bureau of Indian Affairs, the entity that owns and operates the project, continues to not have a long-term plan for rehabilitation nor a short-term plan for rehabilitation. The major rehabilitation efforts that have been undertaken have been led by the Eastern Shoshone and Northern Arapaho Tribes.

The Bureau of Indian Affairs Irrigation staff at Wind River is significantly understaffed and the system is operated inefficiently with only minor necessary improvements. In an effort to provide the required operational and maintenance needs of the system the Tribes have encouraged irrigators in the system to form users associations. These users associations negotiate cooperative assistance agreements, CAAs, with the Bureau of Indian Affairs to assume the operation and maintenance on their designated portion of the system. A percentage of the irrigation assessment is returned to the association to provide funding for operation staff and needed maintenance. Under the CAA the association has seen a dramatic improvement over the overall operation and maintenance of their part of the system compared to the past service provided by the Bureau of Indian Affairs. Nevertheless, the overall project is still in dire need of major improvement.

It is hoped that each association can accumulate a rehabilitation fund that can be leveraged to acquire additional funding from sources such as the Wyoming Water Development Commission. The Eastern Shoshone and Northern Arapaho Tribes strongly endorse the Barrasso amendment, Title IV of S. 715, the Authorized Rural Water Projects Completion Act. The funds that would be provided through this bill would provide for the much needed rehabilitation of the Wind River Indian Irrigation Project that has for decades been neglected by the Bureau of Indian Affairs.

Additionally, these funds could be leveraged to acquire additional funding from the State of Wyoming. While we understand that S. 715 is not pending before the Indian Affairs Committee, the Eastern Shoshone and Northern Arapaho Tribes ask you as individuals to support successfully moving the bill forward.

The Reclamation Fund now has surplus funds in it, certainly more than has been expended in any one year. We live in the middle of one of the Reclamation States. It is really not fair that Indian Irrigation projects have not previously been able to tap into that funding.

The Tribes have compiled a successful track record doing rehabilitation work on the project. In 2004, in an effort to facilitate the rehabilitation of the Wind River Irrigation Project, the Eastern Shoshone and Northern Arapaho Tribes, through the efforts of the Wind River Water Resource Control Board applied to and were granted a $3.5 million grant from the Wyoming Water Development Commission to aid in the rehabilitation of irrigation structures. The State appropriation was a 50 percent grant that required an additional $3.5 million in matching funds before the State funds could be used. Once again through the efforts of the Wind River Water Resource Control Board, in conjunction with the efforts of Senator Mike Enzi, a Federal appropriation of $3.72 million was secured to match the $3.5 million in State funds.

These funding sources were utilized to rehabilitate 15 major structures that were crucial to the operation of the irrigation system and were considered to be in critical need of repair or replacement. The total cost of this phase of the rehabilitation project was $7.7 million. Without the efforts of the Shoshone and Arapaho Tribes, this phase would not have even taken place.

The current Federal and State appropriations have been depleted now, and the Water Resource Control Board is going forward with approaching the State of Wyoming to acquire additional funds for rehabilitation. The Eastern Shoshone and Northern Arapaho Tribes again, once again, endorse the Barrasso amendment to S. 715.

Maintenance fees on the Wind River Irrigation Project continue to rise. And our maintenance continues to decrease. According to a 2008 HKM assessment, the total replacement cost is about $69.6 million. Today those costs are $77.1 million.

I could go on more and more about the Wind River Irrigation Project, but it is clear that the Bureau of Indian Affairs has neglected it over decades. We encourage this Committee to help move S. 715 forward to help with our further irrigation rehab.

Thank you once again for having me, and I look forward to answering your questions.

[The prepared statement of Mr. Cottenoir follows:]

PREPARED STATEMENT OF MITCHEL T. COTTENOIR, TRIBAL WATER ENGINEER, EASTERN SHOSHONE AND NORTHERN ARAPAHO TRIBES OFFICE OF THE TRIBAL WATER ENGINEER

Chairman Tester, Vice Chairman Barrasso and members of the Committee, thank you for inviting me as a representative of the Eastern Shoshone and Northern Arapaho Tribes to appear before you today.

Little has changed on the Wind River Reservation Irrigation Project since the April 2011 Field Hearing held by Senator Barrasso in Riverton, WY. Operation and Maintenance Assessments have continued to rise and deferred maintenance continues to rise as well. The Bureau of Indian Affairs, the entity that owns and operates the project, continues to not have any long term plan for rehabilitation of the Wind River Irrigation Project. The major rehabilitation efforts that have been undertaken have been led by the Eastern Shoshone and Northern Arapaho Tribes, the Wind River Water Resource Control Board and the Office of the Tribal Water Engineer.

The Bureau of Indian Affairs Irrigation staff at the Wind River project is significantly understaffed and the the system is operated inefficiently with only minor necessary maintenance. In an effort to provide the required operational and maintenance needs of the system the Tribes have encouraged irrigators in the system to form water users associations. These associations have negotiated Cooperative Assistance Agreements (CAA) with the Bureau of Indian Affairs to assume the operation and maintenance of their designated portion of the system. A percentage of the irrigation assessment is returned to the association to provide funding for operating staff and needed maintenance. Under the CAA each association has seen a dramatic improvement the overall operation and maintenance of their part of the system compared to the past services provided by the Bureau of Indian Affairs. Nonetheless the overall project is in dire need of major repair.

It is hoped that each association can accumulate a rehabilitation fund that can be leveraged to acquire additional funding from sources such as the Wyoming Water Development Commission. We have had some success in such efforts in recent years.

The Eastern Shoshone and Northern Arapaho Tribes, the Wind River Water Resource Control Board and the Office of the Tribal Water Engineer strongly endorse the Barrasso amendment (title IV) to S. 715, the Authorized Rural Water Projects

Completion Act. The funds that would be provided thru this bill would provide for the much needed rehabilitation of the Wind River Irrigation Project that has for decades been neglected by the Bureau of Indian Affairs. Additionally, these funds could be leveraged to acquire additional funding from the State of Wyoming. While we understand that S.715 in not pending before the Indian Affairs Committee, the Eastern Shoshone and Northern Arapaho Tribes ask for your individual support in successfully moving the bill forward. The Reclamation Fund now has surplus funds in it, certainly more than has ever been expended in any year and we live in the middle of one of the Reclamation States. It is really not fair that Indian Irrigation projects have not previously been able to tap into this fund.

The Tribes have compiled a successful track record doing rehabilitation work on the project. In 2003, the Wyoming Legislature passed House Bill 144 which allowed the Tribes to participate in state funding toward water development projects. That bill was strongly supported by both the Joint Business Council and the Wind River Water Resource Control Board.

In 2004 in an effort to facilitate the rehabilitation of the Wind River Irrigation Project, the Eastern Shoshone and Northern Arapaho Tribes through the efforts of the Wind River Water Resource Control Board applied to and were granted a $3.5M grant from the Wyoming Water Development Commission to aid in the rehabilitation of irrigation structures that were in dire need of repair or replacement. This State Appropriation was a 50 percent grant that required an additional $3.5M in matching funds before the State funds could be used. Once again through the efforts of the Wind River Water Resource Control Board in conjunction with the efforts led by Senator Mike Enzi, a Federal appropriation of $3.72M was secured in 2005 and 2006 as matching funds for the $3.5M in State funds.

These funding sources were utilized to rehabilitate 15 major structures that were crucial to the operation of the irrigation system and were considered to be in critical need of repair or replacement. These structures include: the Johnstown and Lefthand Ditch diversion and waste-way structures on the Big Wind River, the Coolidge Canal—Trout Creek diversion structure, the Mill Creek—Ray Canal Crossing structure, the Ray Canal—South Fork of the Little Wind diversion structure, the Coolidge Canal—Little Wind diversion structure, Ray Canal 11C, 39C and 59C diversion structures, Coolidge Canal 14B diversion structure, the Sub-agency Canal—Little Wind River diversion structure, the North Fork of the Little Wind River diversion chute structure, and the Willow Creek and Meadow Creek diversion structures in the Crowheart area.

Incorporated in the design and construction of the Coolidge and Sub-agency structures are Fish Ladders. In addition to a Fish Ladder, a Fish Screen structure was also designed and constructed on Ray Canal. The fish passage will mitigate the loss of hundreds of thousands of fish to the irrigation system. The fish passage project was a combined effort among the Tribes, the US Fish and Wildlife Service, the Bureau of Indian Affairs, Trout Unlimited and the State of Wyoming.

The total cost of Phase I of the Wind River Irrigation Rehabilitation Project was $7,713,695.

Without the efforts of the Eastern Shoshone and Northern Arapaho Tribes through the Wind River Water Resource Control Board, even these phases of rehabilitation of the Project would not be occurring.

The current Federal and State appropriations are now depleted. The WRWRCB plans on pursuing additional funds from both the Federal Government and the State of Wyoming. The Tribes and the Wind River Water Resource Control Board request the aid and assistance of both Senators Barrasso and Enzi and the Senate Committee on Indian Affairs to help secure future funding for the ongoing rehabilitation of the Wind River Irrigation System. For this reason, the Eastern Shoshone and Northern Arapaho Tribes, the Wind River Water Resource Control Board and the Office of the Tribal Water Engineer again endorse the Barrasso amendment (title IV) to S. 715, the Authorized Rural Water Projects Completion Act. The 38,300 irrigated acres of the Wind River Irrigation Project are assessed Operation and Maintenance Fees to finance the Irrigation Project's operations, maintenance and administrative functions. These O&M assessments have been historically low, but over the past 20 years these rates have risen from a low of $10.90 in 1991 to $22 in 2014. With each irrigation season comes additional assessment costs to cover increased budget shortfalls caused by mandated pay raises for Bureau of Indian Affairs Irrigation Project employees. Even with the rising assessment fees, little rehabilitation efforts have been made.

According to the GAO Report 06–314 dated February 2006, the Wind River Irrigation Project was authorized for construction in 1905 but construction was never completed.

The Wind River Irrigation Project is comprised of 3 storage facilities, 11 canals and 377 miles of canals and laterals. These facilities provide water to 38,300 acres of which 67 percent is Indian owned and 33 percent non-Indian owned.

According to the 1994 Natural Resource Consulting Engineers (NRCE) Project Assessment and Plan, no Project-wide rehabilitation of the delivery system has occurred since the 1930's. According to that study due to deferred maintenance over many years, 60 percent or 1200 structures were in need of repair or replacement and 45 percent or 190 miles of canals and laterals need repair or reconstruction. According to the study structure failures were routine resulting in the progressive loss of control of Project water and that catastrophic failure of segments of the delivery system was imminent. According to the 1994 NRCE Project Assessment and Plan due to the Project's current configuration, it only has 66 acres of irrigated land per mile of canal. In comparison, Midvale Irrigation District has over 160 acres per mile of canal. As a general guideline, the Bureau of Reclamation suggests that irrigation projects, in the region, need at least 140 acres of irrigated land per mile of canal to be economically self sufficient. The study also stated that the resulting poor delivery performance had contributed to a progressive deterioration in crop quality and the water users' ability to pay assessments. It is apparent that the Wind River Irrigation System cannot be considered self sufficient.

The condition of the Wind River Irrigation Project sadly continues to deteriorate and little has changed since the 1994 NRCE Wind River Irrigation Project Assessment, the 2006 GAO Report numbered 06–314 or the 2008 HKM Wind River Irrigation Project Engineering Evaluation and Condition Assessment. The 2008 HKM Wind River Irrigation Project Engineering Evaluation and Condition assessment estimated the costs for needed replacement construction to be $69,640,000. Inflation raises those cost to approximately $77,091,500 in 2014.

Clearly something needs to be done. While we hope the Congress will enact S. 715 with the Barrasso Amendment, we understand the odds of that happening this year are not good. If funds are not made available to deal with the repairs needed, the project will continue to lose water, and both the Indian and non-Indian people who rely on the project, as well as the fisheries impacted by the project, will all suffer. Allowing for congressionally directed appropriations as Senator Enzi was once able to do for us needs to be brought back and the leaders in the highest levels of the Department of the Interior and at OMB need to be forced to own up to what their neglect of this project has caused.

What follows is a report on the Irrigation Rehab Project for which the Tribes have submitted Level II Phase II Storage Site Study Applications to the WWDC. These studies will identify at least 2 suitable storage sites on each of the Big and Little Wind Rivers. The need for additional storage on the Wind River Reservation has been graphically demonstrated during drought years when irrigators have been shut off early in the summer months as early as the first or second week in July. These photos graphically show what progress looks like, i.e., what we can jointly accomplish when we have the funding as well as demonstrate what happens when maintains is deferred and the project is allowed to deteriorate.

In order for the rehabilitation effort to move forward, it will take a united effort from the Eastern Shoshone and Northern Arapaho Tribes, the Bureau of Indian Affairs, the Wyoming Water Development Commission, and our State and Federal Legislators.

Your strong support of the Tribes and their efforts is of the utmost importance. Our efforts will bring much needed relief to both Tribal and non-Tribal irrigators on the Wind River Reservation.

We look forward to working closely with you now and in the future. Thank you for your time and consideration.

Attachments

WIND RIVER IRRIGATION REHAB UPDATE by THE OFFICE OF THE TRIBAL WATER ENGINEER

The Wind River Water Resource Control Board and the Office of the Tribal Water Engineer appreciates this opportunity to up-date the members of the United States Senate Committee on Indian Affairs on the progress of the Wind River Irrigation Rehabilitation Project.

In 2004 the Wyoming State Legislature appropriated $3,500,000 thru the Wyoming Water Development Commission to assist in the rehabilitation of the Wind River Irrigation Project. These funds were matched with two Federal appropriations in 2006 and 2007 totaling $3,722,500. The combined funding was utilized to rehabilitate irrigation structures in critical need of repair. To this date the total estimated cost of rehabilitating the Irrigation Project remains in the $90M range.

Ray Canal Diversion Structure and Fish Passage

During the 2010–2011 and 2011–2012 construction seasons the following rehabilitation project structures were completed:

- Coolidge—Trout Creek Diversion Structure
- Johnstown Diversion Structure
- Lefthand Ditch Diversion and Waste Way Structures
- Ray Canal—Mill Creek Crossing Structure
- Ray Canal Diversion Structure
- Coolidge Canal Diversion Structure
- Ray Canal Fish Screen Structure
- Structures: 39–C, 11–C, 59–C, and 14–B

Total cost of rehabilitating these structures was $5,097,095.

In addition to replacing the Ray and Coolidge Canal diversion structures, fish ladders were installed on both diversion structures to enable aquatic life to migrate the stream above and below the diversion structures. A fish screen structure was also constructed in the Ray Canal down steam of the diversion structure. The fish screen will prevent the loss of thousands of fish to the Ray Canal irrigation system. The fish screen structure was built thru the collaborative efforts of various agencies. Funding partners for the fish passage and screens were: USF&W, Trout Unlimited, the Wyoming Wild Life Trust Fund, BIA Wildlife Resources Branch, the WWDC and the Eastern Shoshone and Northern Arapaho Tribes. These funding partners contributed an additional $720,760.

Ray Canal Fish Screen

The 2013–2014 construction season brought this phase of the Wind River Irrigation Rehabilitation Project to a close. WWDC and Federal Funding have been depleted with the start of the 2014 irrigation season. Projects constructed during this period were:

- North Fork Chute
- Willow Creek Diversion Structure
- Meadow Creek Diversion Structure
- Sub-agency Diversion Structure

The total construction costs of these structures were $2,616,599.29.

48

Sub-agency Diversion Structure

Meadow Creek

Willow Creek

North Fork Chute

It should be noted this rehabilitation project has provided an economic boost to Fremont County, the State of Wyoming and the Wind River Indian Reservation. State and local contractors and sub-contractors have been utilized during the construction projects. These contractors include:

- Inberg-Miller Engineers (Riverton, WY)
- Lowham Walsh LLC (Lander)
- Dowl HKM (Lander)
- High Country Construction (Lander)
- 71 Construction (Riverton)
- Reiman Corp. (Cheyenne)

This phase of the Irrigation Rehab Project has barely scratched the surface of the overall needs of the Wind River Irrigation Project. As stated before the estimated cost of total rehabilitation is in the $90M range. The Office of the Tribal Water Engineer has begun the process of developing a Phase III list of priorities for rehabilitation. This list and a cost estimate will be brought to the WWDC during the next funding cycle, in November of 2014.

Phase III photos of structures on the priority list have been retained in the Committee files

The CHAIRMAN. Thank you, Mitchel, thank you for your testimony. Thank you all for our testimony.

Senator Barrasso?

Senator BARRASSO. Thank you very much, Mr. Chairman. Thanks to each and every one of you for bringing these stories to us today.

If I could ask just a couple of questions, first, Chairman Old Coyote, in your written testimony, you noted that despite some temporary setbacks in improving the Crow Irrigation Project, that ultimately progress is being made in the right direction. You also noted that the improvements to the system did actually provide tangible results.

Can you just tell us a little bit about how your tribal members and the economy can benefit, have benefited or will benefit from the improvements to the Crow Irrigation Project?

Mr. OLD COYOTE. There is a portion in the settlement that anticipates the tribes buying land for farming, taking land into trust, using provisions in the settlement and developing that land for tribally-owned farms. We will be using those provisions as the project develops.

We do not currently anticipate any significant non-tribal development of additional acreage. So that is one of the impacts on the tribe.

Senator BARRASSO. Thank you.

Mr. Cottenoir, last fall we talked a little bit about that amendment, S. 715, to the Authorized Rural Water Projects Completion Act, which would assist in the rehabilitation of Indian irrigation projects. Your written testimony states that the irrigation funding could then be leveraged to access additional funding for rehab and repairs.

Can you just tell us a little bit more about how this rehab would benefit the tribes, the members, the local economies that surround the Wind River Reservation?

Mr. COTTENOIR. Yes, Vice Chairman Barrasso. The funding that we could get through S. 715 could be leveraged through to acquire funds from the State of Wyoming through the Wyoming Water Development Commission. Our previous matching funds were acquired through the efforts of Senator Enzi, that was $3.72 million. We were able to able to match the $3.5 million with the State of Wyoming to acquire the $7.7 million that we used in our irrigation.

Those funds over the past few years have been an economic boost to not only the Wind River Reservation but to Fremont County and the State of Wyoming. We have utilized local contractors that provided all the work, all the contractors were from within the State of Wyoming. Through our TERO ordinance, the contractors had to employ Indian contractors and Indian workers. So that provided dramatic boosts to our economy over that period of five years.

Senator BARRASSO. The other thing that caught my eye when reading your written testimony and also hearing your oral testimony today was how the water users on the Wind River Reservation have formed associations, associations to assume the operation and maintenance of their portion of the Wind River Irrigation System. And the associations, as you said, have seen a dramatic improvement in the overall operation and maintenance of their part of the system compared to the past services from the BIA.

So can you just explain a little why there is such an improvement when the associations take over the operations and the maintenance of the system?

Mr. COTTENOIR. Yes, Senator Barrasso. As you mentioned, the O&M costs on the Wind River continue to rise and the deferred maintenance continues to increase. BIA does little if any maintenance. It is mostly operations. All the funds that they collect go mainly for the statutorily mandated wage increases for BIA personnel.

In our irrigation associations, which the tribes are encouraging to be going out and negotiating more and more cooperative agreements, the BIA collects the O&M still, but then they return a portion of that, probably 50 percent of that, to the association. The association goes out and hires their own operational people and they have their own maintenance schedule. They are able to fund through their own efforts the maintenance necessary on their portion of the irrigation system. And the Crowheart has two of these associations, and we have a Ray Canal Association which was just formed. Since the time of the formation of those groups, there has been a drastic improvement over the services and over the maintenance that has been provided. BIA, through their inefficient and ineffective management and operation, they can't provide those services and they can't provide the maintenance necessary. The CAAs enable the water users to go ahead and take care of their needs, the needs that they see that are needed and the maintenance and operation that the BIA cannot or will not provide.

Senator BARRASSO. Thank you very much. Thank you, Mr. Chairman.

The CHAIRMAN. Thank you. Senator Udall?

Senator UDALL. Thank you, Senator Tester, and thank you for the courtesies on the time here.

Let me thank, first of all, all the witnesses. I think you have given very good testimony on these irrigation issues. The thing that is important here is I think throughout this there is a theme about BIA neglect on these irrigation issues that this Committee needs to take notice of.

I have a couple of comments and then a couple of questions to Governor Paisano. As you mentioned, Governor Paisano, Senator Bingaman had a piece of legislation called the Rio Grande Pueblos Irrigation Infrastructure Improvement Act. We have built on that act in terms of putting in, Senator Heinrich and I, the New Mexico Drought Relief Act. We put that in to address this and other irrigation and water delivery issues. It calls for the reauthorization of Senator Bingaman's act, and an increase in funding for infrastructure. This legislation would also authorize emergency and non-emergency funding to further support water deliveries and irrigation for New Mexico Pueblos and other communities.

I would also like to just mention the Navajo Irrigation Project, which has begun to accumulate a backlog of maintenance, despite being years from completion of the project. This project is vital to the Navajo economic development and is a result of a decades-old agreement with the Federal Government. The project is years behind schedule and this demands the attention of our Committee and the BIA. I would invite my colleagues on the Committee to work with me, to increase appropriations for Pueblo infrastructure and for the Navajo Irrigation Project and other tribal irrigation funding through the Interior Department appropriations.

Now, Governor Paisano, can you just give us a sense of how much of a priority is irrigation infrastructure improvement and related water issues for your administration at Sandia Pueblo and for the other six Middle Rio Grande Pueblos?

Mr. PAISANO. Chairman Tester, Senator Udall, water is such a huge priority. One thing I didn't mention here, because of the sensitivity of time, is related to the cultural aspects of water, what that means to us. My colleague here, Councilwoman Jim, recognized that at the beginning.

You can't even place a value on that culture, the history and the traditions. It is hard to convey in the English language. But besides that, water delivery to our farmers in order to provide food for our community, food for the families, to provide a source of economic development for them, is a priority for the six Pueblos of New Mexico. We consistently are fighting with the BIA. We are caught in the middle between two Federal agencies, that is the Reclamation and BIA. And then another third party, the MRGCD, which is a totally different entity, and our farmers and the Pueblos are caught in the middle.

We are being left out because we are not the ones writing the check. So we typically don't get listened to, so to speak. So it is an uphill battle for us. Over the years it has become a little bit better with the increased involvement with the BIA. But we need funding to help fix the infrastructure in order to get that water delivered to the six Pueblos.

So that is our number one priority right now. Because of the cultural sensitivity of it, providing nutrition for the members of our communities and to also provide a sense of economic development for our farmers in growing higher value crops, such as alfalfa, the sweet sudans, and/or foods like corn, lettuce, tomatoes, chili, et cetera.

Senator UDALL. Thank you, and it is very important, the emphasis on the cultural side of this. You are struggling to maintain your language, you are struggling to maintain your culture. Water is intimate to that. And the production of agricultural products really makes a difference there. I am glad you emphasized that, and the other witnesses did too.

Could you in just a few seconds here, because I am running out of time, give us an idea what you think the BIA could be doing to be more supportive of your situation? They are a key agency here.

Mr. PAISANO. One key thing probably would be the instability of the staff. Over the last five years, we have gone through three designated engineers. That is the individual who is assigned by the BIA to help coordinate this water delivery and maintenance of our infrastructure with the MRGCD. There is a lot of turnover in the BIA, and that doesn't help us. That is probably one key priority that they could help us with. Obviously the funding already mentioned.

Senator UDALL. Well, we have to do everything we can, I think, Senator Tester, to help push the BIA to get more involved in all these irrigation situations. Thank you so much for bringing the attention to this. I really, really appreciate it.

The CHAIRMAN. Thank you, Senator Udall, for your questions, and thank you for your interest in the issue. A lot of these problems aren't going to be solved unless we appropriate the kind of money we need to be able to support the projects.

You had a question or comment?

Ms. JIM. Mr. Chairman, I would like to make a correction to my testimony.

The CHAIRMAN. Sure.

Ms. JIM. I stated $12 million. It is supposed to read $12 billion. I want you to excuse me for that.

The CHAIRMAN. A small bit.

[Laughter.]

Ms. JIM. Thank you for allowing me to make that correction.

The CHAIRMAN. Absolutely. I have a few questions here. Chairman Old Coyote, your testimony stated that a couple years back there was negotiating between yourselves and the Bureau of Rec since your tribal water settlement has been approved. A couple of things, what kind of issues came up, but more importantly, what is your relationship with the Bureau of Rec?

Mr. OLD COYOTE. Thank you, Chairman Tester. There were a lot of issues, some technical oversight issues, some on budget. The biggest issue I mentioned in my testimony initially was that they were requiring the tribe to advance all the money from our general fund budget, which was nearly impossible. These have largely been resolved, and now we have the master plan, which we are hoping, we expect to have approved very soon. With a big ramp-up in construction right now, there is close to 28 construction jobs. And with the master plan being approved, that will ramp up to like 50 for the next three or four years.

So our relationship with BIA, we have always had an excellent relationship with Mike Connor. He has been one of the most pragmatic and decisive people we have dealt with. Our relations with the region have not always been as good, but currently are in a fairly good place and we hope they stay there.

The CHAIRMAN. The Crow irrigation project was included in the 2006 GAO report, which stated the project had over $50 million in deferred maintenance back in 2006. The maintenance for the project was included in the tribal settlement that was passed since then.

Based on your tribe's experience of coupling the irrigation infrastructure with water settlements, I just want to make it clear, I think you addressed this in your testimony, but I want you to make it clear, what advice do you have for us lawmakers as far as considering laws that would improve tribal access to water and coupling maintenance with water settlements, for example?

Mr. OLD COYOTE. Chairman Tester, thank you. First, the future water settlements must include a sufficient level of mandatory appropriations. The Crow Tribe, the Crow Nation is extremely fortunate that our settlement included mandatory funding, thanks to you and Senator Baucus for seeing the need there for mandatory funding.

Another aspect of funding that Congress should include is the flexibility to shift funding among relevant accounts. Right now we have a CIP and MR9, both accounts shifting among relevant accounts. That is another area that we would make suggestions as well.

The CHAIRMAN. Okay. Question for you, Governor Paisano, and thank you, Chairman Old Coyote. Your testimony states that the BIA pays the Middle Rio Grande Conservancy District for the operations and maintenance of the irrigation system on Pueblo lands. But that same conservancy district has not done a very good job of treating Pueblo lands equally with others. Do they give you any reasons for that?

Mr. PAISANO. Chairman Tester, quite honestly, no. The BIA has appropriated about a million dollars a year for the services. The BIA automatically takes off about $150,000 of that for salaries, I guess, for the designated engineer. So what is left to negotiate for those services is about $850,000. Whatever is left is very little, typically, in order to improve our infrastructure. But it is kind of a give and take. It is all relationship building in New Mexico. And we don't have a good working relationship with the MRGCD at the upper echelon. We do with the on the ground folks.

But the on the ground folks, when we ask them, we literally, and I have seen it happen, bribe them to, we will go out and get them breakfast burritos, we will take them doughnuts, and so forth, and they'll mow our irrigation ditches. That is literally what it has come down to, is building that relationship.

But when they get upset at you, they say, sorry, we haven't been paid, we are not going to cut the weeds, we are not going to fix the ditches. It is quite a mess, quite honestly.

The CHAIRMAN. Is there any accounting of Middle Rio Grande Conservancy District's use of the funds that they get from the BIA?

Mr. PAISANO. We have started to build our own. That is something we have asked to have done. To my knowledge, I don't believe it has been officially. We take photographs, we mark the date that they are out there doing some work for us. And we then give that information to the BIA. Then we somewhat have an internal document that we will sign off on before the BIA will pay the funds to MRGCD for the services rendered.

But if they are not paid, once again that goes back to, hey, we did this much, and BIA says, oh, no, you only did a quarter of a mile, then they stop all work on all the Pueblos until they get paid.

The CHAIRMAN. Thank you, and thank you for your testimony also.

Councilwoman Jim, it is good to have you here too. Your testimony indicates that the Wapato Irrigation Project was erroneously listed as a self-sustaining project by the DOI back in the 1980s. So could I ask you, even if we come up with the funding to fix the deferred maintenance issue, the project itself would not be collecting enough O&M fees to keep the maintenance up to date. Is that a correct assessment or am I off on that one?

Ms. JIM. No, it isn't, because the Wapato Irrigation Project is on the Yakama Reservation. We do have our lands that are owned by tribal members that are leased. But being that they are fractionated, then you run into the incapability of leasing that land, because maybe the biggest share landowner has expired and then so it is in probate. Then you have probate upon probate.

The CHAIRMAN. So I would assume you guys are involved with the buyback program?

Ms. JIM. We did put a letter of intent in. But we were informed by Genevieve or GG, whatever the lady that is in charge now, not to do anything for 60 months.

The CHAIRMAN. We will follow up on that, too. It is an important issue for tribes across this Country and it was set up to help remedy situations exactly like you have. I say that as I am looking at the Crow and they are in the same program, probably all of you are, quite frankly.

You have a number of projects, as per your testimony. And you have a large number of acres that aren't irrigated on your reservation. If we fix the deferred maintenance, would that save enough water to open up some more acres?

Ms. JIM. Yes, it would. Like I stated in my testimony, there have been numerous studies on all Indian irrigation projects. During the last study, they said it would cost approximately $136 million to $276 million just to do the rehab of Wapato Irrigation Project. And this wasn't even recent.

The CHAIRMAN. Well, thank you for being here today, thank you for your testimony. We very much appreciate it.

Mitchel, your testimony discussed some of the construction projects to repair the Wind River Irrigation Project in the last 10 years, after getting some funding from the State and the Feds. Can you estimate how many jobs this funding helped to create?

Mr. COTTENOIR. Senator Tester, I believe that it is in the order of 100 jobs that were created for construction people. We employed five different engineering firms to do design work.

The CHAIRMAN. Over how long of a period?

Mr. COTTENOIR. Since 2006, I believe, is when the design work began. The construction phase just concluded this past spring.

The CHAIRMAN. Okay. Could you discuss the impact that the Wind River Irrigation Project has on both tribal and the non-tribal community, both, what impact does it have?

Mr. COTTENOIR. The impact on both tribal and non-tribal are the same. We are pretty much a checkerboard area, where tribal and non-tribal irrigators are side by side. So both tribal and non-tribal irrigators are dependent on this inefficient and mismanaged system that we have had for decades. It is just a hardship for everyone, tribal and non-tribal. It doesn't distinguish between tribal and non-tribal.

The CHAIRMAN. This question is for all of you. It is just a question on who benefits from these irrigation systems. Is it the tribes? I am talking about the tribal government and the tribes. Are they able to take advantage of irrigation systems and improvements? Or does the primary advantage go to individual farmers that may either have or lease tribal lands?

Mr. OLD COYOTE. The benefit is to landowners, it increases the value of their lands. Also the farmers and ranchers, for the crops and farming, it increases their farming as well. So the benefit goes to the farmer. The reason why I say farmer is that a lot of times, the landowners are tribal members and the farmers are non-Indians. So it benefits both.

The CHAIRMAN. Okay. Governor Paisano, how about in your neck of the woods?

Mr. PAISANO. Chairman Tester, in New Mexico, in the Middle Rio Grande Valley, probably, I have to say that the individuals that benefit the most are the non-Pueblo irrigators. You see in the pictures that I provided to this Committee, because the infrastructure is so outdated and not maintained within the reaches of the Pueblo, the water just goes straight through and then everything is being cleaned and maintained and so forth to non-irrigators. And whatever water we don't use, it gets dumped back into the Middle Rio Grande River to help support the silvery minnow, which is under the Endangered Species Act, and then it goes further south to a reservoir called Elephant Butte, that then goes to Texas to help with the compact routine, Colorado, New Mexico and Texas.

The CHAIRMAN. Do you have additional acres that you could put under irrigation if there was water available to irrigate?

Mr. PAISANO. Yes.

The CHAIRMAN. Councilwoman Jim, same question. Who gets the advantage out of the improvements? Is it the tribes, the members, the farmers, who is it in Washington?

Ms. JIM. All of the above.

The CHAIRMAN. Really? Okay.

Ms. JIM. Yes, because the Tribe owns a lot of land, tribal tracts. We still have a lot of Indian landowners. And we have a lot of farmers in the Yakima Valley.

The CHAIRMAN. Mitchel, how about you?

Mr. COTTENOIR. Senator Tester, I think I agree, all of the above are the ones that get the advantage to improvements on our irrigation system. At Wind River we have a water code that has 15 beneficial uses, and they are outlined in the code. It goes all the way from domestic to cultural to irrigation. But each and every one of those uses are held at the same priority.

I think that ultimately, right now, the people that most benefit from our irrigation system are the downstream water users, the water users off the reservation. Because of our inefficient system, the deferred maintenance, the lack of storage, we can't use the water when we have it. So the actual beneficiaries of our water at the present are the downstream users off the reservation.

The CHAIRMAN. Once again, thank you all. We appreciate your testimony and appreciate the answers to the questions today, and I appreciate your making the trek here to Washington, D.C. Note that the hearing record will be open for two weeks from today for any additions.

With that, this hearing is adjourned. Thank you all.

[Whereupon, at 3:50 p.m., the hearing was adjourned.]

APPENDIX

PREPARED STATEMENT OF HON. EDWARD T. BEGAY, CHAIRMAN OF THE BOARD OF DIRECTORS, NAVAJO AGRICULTURAL PRODUCTS INDUSTRY

Introduction

Good afternoon Chairman Tester, Vice Chairman Barrasso, and members of the Senate Committee on Indian Affairs. I am Edward T. Begay and I am the Chairman of the Board of Directors for the Navajo Agricultural Products Industry (NAPI), an agricultural company chartered under the laws of the Navajo Nation. I am pleased to submit this Statement for the Record relating to the Committee's Oversight Hearing titled, "Irrigation Projects in Indian Country."

Background on the Navajo Indian Irrigation Project

In 1868, the United States Senate ratified a Treaty with the Navajo Nation which recognized the importance of agriculture to the self-sufficiency of the Navajo people.

In 1962, after ten years of intense negotiations between the Navajo Nation, the State of New Mexico, and the United States, Congress authorized the Navajo Indian Irrigation Project ("NIIP," Pub.L.87–483), to fulfill, in part, the United States treaty obligations to supply water and a farming operation for the Navajo Nation. The legislative history, as well as the text of the 1962 statute, makes clear the Federal commitment to build an 110,630-acre, irrigated-farm. The 1962 Act authorized $135 million for these purposes. In 1970, Congress amended the Act and increased the authorized appropriations to $206 million. In 2005, the Bureau of Indian Affairs (BIA) indexed this figure to 2005 dollars and estimated that there might be as much as $229 million in funding that could be appropriated without the need for a fresh authorization.

It was originally estimated that the NIIP would be completed in about twelve years, in tandem with a companion project—the San Juan-Chama Project. The Navajo Nation made valuable concessions in exchange for the NIIP, allowing water from the San Juan Basin (to which the Navajo Nation had valid claims) to be transported to the Rio Grande Basin in New Mexico, for the substantial benefit of non-Navajos. The San-Juan Chama Project was completed in 1976, and the residents and businesses of the Rio Grande Basin have been enjoying the benefits of the bargain for nearly forty years.

The NIIP construction began in 1964 and fifty-two years later, only seventy percent has been completed and, as one would expect, the NIIP's physical infrastructure has begun to fall into serious disrepair.

NAPI's Operations and Economic Importance

On April 16, 1970, NAPI was established by the Navajo Nation Council as a tribal enterprise to manage and operate the NIIP. The idea behind NAPI was to both manage the NIIP and to create economic opportunities for the Navajo people and to build a foundation of commitment, pride, and dedication to their Nation.

Today, NAPI operates a 75,000-acre farm in Farmington, New Mexico, generates $69 million in revenues to the Navajo Nation and San Juan County, employs more than 417 people in the Four Corners Area, and purchases tens of millions of dollars in goods and services both locally and across the Nation. In its operations, NAPI has stressed the use of the state-of-the-art technology and environmentally-friendly practices. NAPI's agribusiness features state-of-the-art farming equipment, including high-tech radio control, and a computerized center pivot irrigation system that reduces operational costs and efficiently manages water resources.

NAPI produces premier "Navajo Pride" brand agricultural products, including alfalfa, corn, wheat and small grains, potatoes, and pinto beans. NAPI also operates a flour mill and leases land for cattle grazing, and specialty crops, including pumpkins, popcorn, and chipper potatoes used for potato chips. Our products have earned the distinction of being "New Mexico Grown" by the New Mexico Department of Agriculture.

Through its Operation & Maintenance Division, NAPI manages the operation and maintenance of the NIIP pursuant to Pub.L.93–638 (Indian Self-Determination and Education Assistance Act), including Operations and Maintenance (O&M), On-Farm Development (OFD), and Agricultural Testing Research Laboratory. While the Bureau of Reclamation, a contractor to the BIA, is responsible for the planning, design, and construction of the NIIP, the BIA has the sole responsibility, including funding requirements, to complete the NIIP.

NIIP Funding Inadequacies

Annual funding for the NIIP O&M was approximately $26 million per year during the Clinton Administration and $14 million during the Bush Administration. Despite promises of unconditional support by the Obama Administration, the budget for the NIIP O&M has been reduced by more than $9 million to a paltry $4 million for the past three fiscal years. The Fiscal Year 2015 budget request includes $3.384 million for the NIIP.

The NAPI Board believes the NIIP O&M funding is wholly inadequate. This level of funding creates a large deferred maintenance backlog. The BIA Irrigation O&M account receives approximately $11 million annually and is used primarily for court-mandated payments, statutory requirements, and water storage costs. Currently, as much as one-third of the $3.384 million NIIP O&M funding pays for electricity for pumping.

NAPI is currently facing an urgent dilemma with the NIIP's 3500 linear foot main canal which requires concrete canal lining replacement and drainage embankment repairs. The NAPI Board has urged the BIA to address these matters to prevent a possible catastrophic failure of the main canal during normal operations, which would result in a failure to deliver water to most of the NAPI farming land.

The Authorized Rural Water Projects Completion Act (S. 715)

In April 2013, former Senator Max Baucus (D–MT) introduced the *Authorized Rural Water Projects Completion Act* (S. 715). The measure establishes, in the U.S. Department of the Treasury, a Reclamation Rural Water Construction Fund. An amendment sponsored by Vice Chairman Barrasso added three additional accounts: the Rural Water Project Account, the Indian Irrigation Account, and the Reclamation Infrastructure and Settlement Implementation Account.

S. 715 directs the Secretary of the Treasury to transfer $150 million and any interest earned from the existing Reclamation Fund into the proposed fund annually through 2035. This amount includes annual funding of $80 million for rural water projects, $35 million for Indian reclamation infrastructure and settlement claims, and $35 million for Indian irrigation projects. The bill authorizes appropriations of annual deposited amounts plus earned interest to complete underfunded rural water projects, settles Indian water claims, and maintains irrigation projects on tribal lands. Indian irrigation projects that have not been funded for the last fifteen years would be given a priority.

In addition, S. 715 directs the Secretary of the Interior to consult with tribal governments and conduct a study that evaluates options for improving programmatic, project management, and performance of irrigation projects managed and operated by the BIA.

The NAPI Board strongly supports S. 715 and urges the Committee to support passage of the bill in the 114th Congress. Further, we wish to thank Vice Chairman Barrasso for his support in proposing a strong tribal amendment to S. 715.

Conclusion

The history of Federal funding and support for the NIIP and related activities reveals that partial and delayed funding has resulted and continues to result in delayed or derailed economic opportunities, job creation, and chronic problems in maintaining physical infrastructure and irrigation equipment.

This concludes my written statement. Thank you for providing me the opportunity to submit this Statement for the Record.

————

PREPARED STATEMENT OF HON. FRED S. VALLO, GOVERNOR, PUEBLO OF ACOMA

The people of the Pueblo of Acoma are residents of the longest continuously occupied community in the United States. For centuries, our people have relied upon traditional farming as a means of survival and as a deeply held cultural belief. Crops like traditional Acoma white corn are used in religious ceremonies. As the Committee is aware, torrential rains and floods during 2010, 2011, 2013, and 2014 resulted in serious damage to our irrigation facilities. These environmental catastrophes paired with years of inadequate maintenance to existing structures have created serious problems with diversions along the system. We provide this comment in strong support of significant funding to restore and renovate Pueblo irrigation ditches.

Anzac Irrigation Ditch was significantly damaged by flooding events, and we have since struggled to initiate and complete repairs under Force Account while coordinating traditional irrigation events and usage with seasonal restrictions and other flood disaster events. Unfortunately, the continual onslaught of environmental events along with other issues have resulted in unavoidable delays to our repairs, which continually compound the problem of irrigation water delivery and progressing damage. In April 2014, we contracted repair services with a priority schedule to make full repair and restoration. Concerns over potential quantity and unit cost overruns were brought to the attention of all participants, including the New Mexico Department of Homeland Security and Emergency Management (DHSEM).

Ditch cleanup and lining removal revealed damage and repairs well beyond the original FEMA scope of work. Once the sediment was removed from ditches, it was apparent much of the damage sustained was below the sediment deposit and normal operational flow level. There is also extensive erosion behind the concrete lining that is minimally accounted for. Once major cleaning and demolition work was completed, a new estimate of the final damage was determined. Unfortunately, the damage repairs and costs are substantially more than the original PW 370 scope of work.

The use of irrigation water is critical to Acoma Pueblo's inherent right as the original and first users of area waters. There is a decades-old water litigation court case *State v. KerrMcGee* that is ongoing; in light of that case, it is essential that Acoma continue to demonstrate the continued use of waters to farm our lands. Without this ability, non-Acoma water users will increase their use and share of water, which will negatively impact Acoma Pueblo for issues that are beyond the Pueblo's control. Lack of maintenance and environmental catastrophes have resulted in the poor condition of our irrigation system today.

The Acoma Pueblo irrigation system is a traditional, cultural, sacred site. It is 47.9 miles in length. Every year, traditional irrigation Ditch Bosses are appointed by our traditional leaders and male members of the community are required to perform seasonal work to clean and maintain the ditch using only hand tools. Ditch work is a community service. Minimal federal and non-federal funds are used only to purchase propane and hand tools. Approximately 85 percent of the irrigation system is lined with concrete and is currently under a phased assessment project to address the issues outlined above. Immediate funding is needed to complete the assessment project, and to thereafter improve and repair the 47.9 miles of traditional irrigation ditches.

Clearly, the Pueblo of Acoma, along with other pueblos in New Mexico, have a great need for funding to apply to irrigation projects. These projects generate jobs and profits not only for tribal members, but for non-members as well. Acoma urges Congress to appropriate the funds needed for these culturally essential and agriculturally necessary projects.

Thank you for your time and consideration, we would be pleased to answer any questions you may have regarding this comment.

PREPARED STATEMENT OF HON. J. MICHAEL CHAVARRIA, GOVERNOR, SANTA CLARA PUEBLO

The people of the Santa Clara Pueblo are the original occupants of what is now Rio Arriba County, New Mexico; our Pueblo currently numbers approximately 3,500. Water plays a major cultural role in our beliefs, and we continue to be reliant on traditional farming and agricultural practices as well. As the Committee is aware, our Pueblo faces a number of issues stemming from the Las Conchas fire. This environmental disaster paired with years of inadequate maintenance to the existing structure has created serious problems with diversions along the system. We provide this comment in strong support of significant funding to restore and renovate Pueblo irrigation ditches.

First, the main ditch inlet from the Rio Grande River must be reconstructed to divert water to Santa Clara's irrigation ditches. Years of upstream flooding has damaged the structure beyond simple repairs; the approximate cost to adequately construct the project is $226,575. Monthly maintenance of the river channel to maintain proper water flow will be tribally funded. However, major maintenance like tree removal and concrete repairs, which have an annual cost of $110,000, lack funding.

Regarding the Canyon Ditch/Guachupangue, this diversion was destroyed by flooding subsequent to the Las Conchas fires. Approximately 1,000 feet of underground irrigation pipe, repairs to the irrigation diversion, and the clearing of 22 culverts from the canyon head gate through the Pueblo and to the south fields have been funded.

Clearing the sediment from the canyon irrigation diversion has only been funded once, despite it being necessary monthly maintenance. It is currently also funded by Santa Clara. The Guachpanque earthen ditch was destroyed; as a result, at least one apple orchard has been lost by the Pueblo. Funding is needed for the annual and monthly maintenance of the Guachpanque ditch.

A culvert at the Rio Grande River has been excavated and cleared by a contractor at the River Ditch. A survey of the ditch has been tentatively funded by the United States Department of Agriculture, but is not yet confirmed. River Ditch starts just south of Santa Clara Creek at the Rio Grande, and runs south for approximately 3 miles. The survey is needed to determine the elevation and slope of the ditch to determine if water will flow, or if additional work is needed.

Santa Clara Pueblo also has a need for funding to hire a seasonal ditch caretaker and 6 to 8 temporary laborers for six-week periods to clear brush, and dig ditches and culverts. These positions are currently funded by the Pueblo. Some specific equipment is needed as well, including a wheeled excavator, to dredge the river and canyon diversions for adequate flow throughout the season, as well as a farm tractor and mower to keep the ditches clear. The latter equipment has been partially funded.

The Main Ditch has yet to be completed—approximately 2 miles must be relined with concrete at an estimated cost of $580,000. This project is not funded. Additionally, the Pueblo Ditch has smaller culverts that are in need of replacement at a cost of $250,000.

Clearly, Santa Clara Pueblo, along with other pueblos along the Rio Grande, have a great need for funding to apply to irrigation projects. These projects generate jobs and profits not only for tribal members, but for non-members as well. Santa Clara urges Congress to appropriate the funds needed for these culturally essential and agriculturally necessary projects.

Thank you for your time and consideration, we would be pleased to answer any questions you may have regarding this comment.

––––––––

PREPARED STATEMENT OF HON. CLEMENT J. FROST, CHAIRMAN, SOUTHERN UTE INDIAN TRIBE

On behalf of the Southern Ute Indian Tribe (the Tribe), I am pleased to submit this statement for the record regarding the Committee on Indian Affairs' September 10, 2014, Oversight Hearing on Irrigation Projects in Indian Country.

The purpose of the Oversight Hearing was to receive testimony from federal officials and tribal leaders on the current state of Indian irrigation projects and the financial resources required to rehabilitate and maintain them. The hearing was conducted in the context of bills pending in the House (H.R. 4420) and Senate (S. 715) known as the *Authorized Rural Water Projects Completion Act.* The Tribe is greatly interested in promoting progress to resolve issues of irrigation project deterioration that are a part of the bills' intent, and wishes to provide its perspectives on these important matters.

The Tribe is heartened that the Congress continues to deliberate the best method for the United States to meet its obligation to work with tribes to resolve an issue of great importance for many of the western Indian tribes. Our Tribe has a particular interest in this issue because the Pine River Indian Irrigation Project (PRIIP) on the Southern Ute Indian Reservation has suffered many decades of neglect and mis-management. Wholly inadequate management of the PRIIP by the U.S. Bureau of Indian Affairs has resulted in a rehabilitation and maintenance backlog variously estimated at between $20 million and $60 million.

The PRIIP has been an important part of the economy and culture of the local Indian and non-Indian community since the late 1800s. Its continued deterioration through the decades has caused economic hardship for both Indians and non-Indians. The project long ago reached a point where conditions created a disincentive for aggressively practicing agriculture. Now, as the Tribe pursues greater efforts to maintain a diversified economy, the state of the PRIIP is a major impediment to economic progress.

The disrepair of the system has still not been adequately catalogued but the following illustrate the system's deplorable condition:

- only an estimated 15 percent of the project's 175 miles of canals can be considered in good condition;
- some of the project's major diversion structures date to the 1930s, with no major rehabilitation or improvements since the 1960s;
- an estimated 40 percent of the project's irrigable acreage is not being irrigated, and a significant amount of that simply cannot be irrigated given the current state of the project;
- the project's largest canal, serving over 4,500 acres of Indian and non-Indian land, has breached twice in less than a year and is only delivering water due to temporary, stop-gap measures;
- dozens of smaller drop structures constructed pre-1920s have collapsed and simply been abandoned;
- many newer structures have already failed due to erosion, poor design, and poor maintenance;
- ditches have been abandoned and lands that were previously irrigated have become derelict, requiring costly rehabilitation; and
- erosion has created miles of incised canals and ditches where elevated headgates no longer allow for the diversion of water to lands that historically were irrigated.

The vast amount of work that is needed to even bring the system to functionality is staggering.

While the Tribe has worked with Congress in the past on PRIIP-specific legislation, at this time we are strongly supportive of the tribal-specific planning and funding approach outlined in the Senate version of the pending legislation, which includes amendments offered by Vice Chairman Barrasso. The Tribe believes this approach can be part of the way forward in addressing the problems of the PRIIP.

In addition to our Tribe's pressing need on its own Reservation, we strongly support and advocate for a system-wide solution to this issue. Furthermore, we believe that the solution to the problem of irrigation project rehabilitation, maintenance, and continued operation must be based on sound planning intended to create long-term agricultural sustainability and economic viability. Only with a clear financial basis, and with commitment from both the United States and the tribes, can these issues be resolved in a manner that prevents this from continuing to be a perpetual burden for the United States and the Tribes.

The Tribe supports both the House and Senate legislation, and strongly endorses S.715 with the Barrasso language included and encourages Congress to commit to working with affected tribes to meet its obligation to resolve this long-standing problem.

I thank you for considering these comments and would be happy to elaborate on the Tribe's experience and perspectives on irrigation projects in general and the PRIIP in particular.

PREPARED STATEMENT OF HON. RONALD TRAHAN, CHAIRMAN, CONFEDERATED SALISH
AND KOOTENAI TRIBES

Dear Senator Tester:

The Confederated Salish and Kootenai Tribes of the Flathead Nation located in northwestern Montana are pleased to present testimony about the Indian Irrigation Project located on our Reservation.

First of all, we have completed negotiations with the United States, Department of the Interior, and the State of Montana on a Proposed Reserved Water Rights Compact. The Proposed Compact was presented to the 2013 Montana Legislature, but failed in Committee. We anticipate that a very similar Proposed Compact will be presented in the 2015 Legislature and if that Compact is adopted we will participate in the established process for presenting the Compact to the United States Congress for approval and for a Federal Contribution to Settlement. Consequently, we do not present testimony at this time on the Flathead Indian Irrigation Project infrastructure (which is critically deteriorated), but do present testimony on the BIA Safety of Dams Program, which receives separate Federal funding, and remains an integral part of the Flathead Indian Irrigation Project.

The Safety of Dams Program was compacted from the Bureau of Indian Affairs in the 1980's. There are 15 high hazard dams on the Flathead Reservation and two which are outside the exterior boundaries of the Reservation which are monitored and rehabilitated when they become safety hazards to the public. The dams on the Flathead Reservation were originally constructed as part of the Flathead Indian Irrigation Project. Some of the dams are greater than 100 years old.

The majority of dams on the Flathead Reservation are in varied states of disrepair and therefore unsafe. Some dams have recently gone through partial rehabilitation upgrades, but this "band aid" approach to an inherently unsafe facility continues to leave the public at risk. To properly rehabilitate all of the dams on the Flathead Reservation additional access to funding is needed. It is very costly to perform rehabilitation projects on these facilities because they are very complex and extremely large in scope.

The Bureau of Indian Affairs currently has an annual operations and maintenance budget of $20 million, which is thinly spread across the 136 dams in their inventory. Of these 136 dams, 12.5% are located on the Flathead Reservation.

To bring all of the Flathead dams into a sufficiently safe condition, the estimated cost for administration, operations/maintenance, engineering design and construction is far in excess of $100 million. Due to the rapidly increasing cost of heavy civil construction, this increase needs to happen in the near future as the costs will continue to climb, further exacerbating the problem.

To fail to address the problem of deteriorating dams on the Flathead Reservation, is to fail to address a natural resources key responsibility acknowledged in the Trust Commission Report dated December 2013. This report acknowledged that the management of irrigation projects and associated water resources is a trust responsibility.

Because dams located within Indian Irrigation Projects receive separate and distinct Federal funding, and because addressing dam deficiencies and safety is a trust responsibility, we ask you to include and increase dam safety funding in any legislation proposed.

Thank you for the opportunity to present this testimony.

PREPARED STATEMENT OF HON. MARCELINO AGUINO, GOVERNOR, OHKAY OWINGEH

Chairman Tester, Vice Chairman Barrasso and members of the Committee, thank you for the opportunity to provide written testimony for the recent oversight hearing on irrigation projects in Indian Country. I am providing these comments on behalf of Ohkay Owingeh.

Ohkay Owingeh is located 25 miles north of Santa Fe, New Mexico, at the confluence of the Rio Grande and the Rio Chama. The Pueblo Grant is within our ancestral lands. Our people have been diverting water and capturing rain water for crops for more than 1000 years. Archeologists have found our ancestors' irrigated agricultural fields dating to the 12th century. Our name, Ohkay Owingeh, is Tewa for "place of the strong people", a truly fitting name to be sure. Ohkay Owingeh is the home of the leader of the Pueblo revolt of 1680, Po'pay. Today, Po'pay is one of only seven Native Americans honored in the U.S. Capitol with a statue in the National Statuary Hall Collection.

For all of these centuries and relatively until recent times, the Pueblo was able to rely upon a clean, and sufficient supply of water. Population increases, an increasing demand for water, water quality concerns, and drought have caused our water supplies to become less reliable. Our ability to maintain our homeland for the future for Ohkay Owingeh people depends on our ability to protect our culture and livelihood, maintain our traditions and ceremonies, protect our rivers, wetlands and lands, and develop our economy. A healthy homeland can only be attained through the continued availability of an adequate supply of safe and clean water. As we have for centuries, the Pueblo continues to rely on irrigated agriculture as a way of life and a key part of our economy. Effective, reliable irrigation projects are essential for economic development both for the Pueblo and for our neighbors, the non-Indian communities that surround us.

Unfortunately, the condition of water and irrigation projects in Indian Country is deteriorating every day. A 2006 Government Accountability Office (GAO) study found that irrigation projects in Indian Country had hundreds of millions of dollars in deferred maintenance costs. There exists a current backlog in maintenance of approximately $598 million for 15 projects. And, because maintenance is being deferred, the infrastructure is falling further into disrepair all across Indian Country.

There is legislation that would begin to address this problem. But much more will need to be done. We support Chairman Tester's bill, the Authorized Rural Water Project Completion Act (S. 715) as well as Senator Udall and Senator Heinrich's drought relief bill (S. 2470) which contain language reauthorizing the Pueblo Irrigation Infrastructure Improvement Act. Unfortunately, these two pieces of legislation will not fix a problem that has been allowed to worsen with years of deferred maintenance costs and severe federal budget cuts. As a sovereign government, Ohkay Owingeh is ultimately responsible to protect and care for the Ohkay Owingeh people. Consequently, we work closely with our non-Indian neighbors, the acequia associations, to do everything we can to maintain irrigation ditch systems that, in some instances, are hundreds of years old.

Ohkay Owingeh is in active discussions with the State of New Mexico, the United States, Santa Clara Pueblo, the City of Espanola, and multiple acequia associations to confirm our right to sufficient water to meet our current and future needs while also protecting the existing uses of our neighbors. We are currently using surface water for irrigation of crops and pasturelands, and to restore native plants and the wetlands of the Rio Grande bosque. Our source of water for domestic, commercial and municipal uses is groundwater. The aquifer underlying the Grant may have unacceptable levels of natural toxins such as arsenic. The Pueblo cannot rely upon that groundwater to meet its future needs without thoroughly analyzing the water quality, and the economic feasibility of using it. It will require several hundred thousand dollars to assess the groundwater's quality and quantity. Those are funds the Pueblo does not have—Ohkay Owingeh looks to its trustee, the United States, for assistance in analyzing its groundwater resource. Our Grant is only a small part of Ohkay Owingeh's ancestral lands and having safe groundwater is essential to our economic security.

For many years the Pueblo has been restoring the Rio Grande bosque for cultural, ceremonial and environmental purposes. It is critical that we return the River's natural flow patterns while removing non-native species while also creating a native habitat for all native, and listed endangered species in order to rehabilitate the bosque.

Water is essential to life for all of us. For Ohkay Owingeh, water is woven through every part of our lives—it is necessary for our ceremonies, is a part of our traditions, and is central to the Pueblo's ability to achieve economic self-sufficiency. The State of New Mexico is deeply committed to quantifying the water rights of all of its citizens. It has commenced litigation to determine the Pueblo's water rights. We must respond. We have made two commitments in that response: that we will ensure that our people have a safe, clean, reliable and sufficient water for the future, and that our neighbors, the non-Indians who live with us in these lands, will be able to continue their existing uses of water. To achieve both of these goals, it is essential that a federal negotiating team be appointed to provide the expertise and resources needed to resolve these complex issues in a timely and cost-efficient manner. The commitment by the U.S. government of sufficient resources to achieve this fair and reasonable settlement is considerably more economical than assigning government resources to years of litigation of multiple cases in which Ohkay Owingeh must assert water rights claims.

In summary, Ohkay Owingeh supports these bills, and supports the efforts of members of Congress to attend to the woefully neglected water supply systems of Indian country.

Thank you for this opportunity to provide testimony on behalf of Ohkay Owingeh for the record.

———

YAKAMA RESERVATION
IRRIGATION DISTRICT
PO BOX 1689
YAKIMA WA 98907

September 2, 2014

Mr. Michael Black
Bureau of Indian Affairs
MS-4606
1849 C Street, N.W.
Washington, D.C. 20240

Mr. David Shaw
Superintendent-Yakama Agency
Bureau of Indian Affairs
401 Fort Road
Po Box 632
Toppenish, WA 98948

Mr. Stanley M. Speaks
Bureau of Indian Affairs
Northwest Regional Director
911 NE. 11th Avenue
Portland, OR 97232-4169

Mr. Jeffrey Harlan
Bureau of Indian Affairs
Portland Regional Office
911 NE 11th Avenue
Portland, OR 97232-4169

Mr. Travis Teegarden
Agricultural Engineer
BIA Division of Water & Power
2021 4th Avenue North, #415
Billings, MT 59101

Re: Wapato Irrigation Project

Gentlemen:

Thank you for giving the board members of Yakama Reservation Irrigation District the opportunity to meet with all of you on August 13, 2014. Your time and attention to this important project is very much appreciated.

As you now know, the Yakima Valley is one of Washington State's most productive and diverse agricultural areas. The Wapato Irrigation Project ("WIP") provides critical irrigation water to over 100,000 acres to non-tribal irrigators consisting of landowners and lessees of tribal parcels on the Yakama Indian Reservation. It is an important water resource to the Yakama Tribe and to non-Indian fee land owners, providing essential water for crops and energy generation. For decades, the WIP has deteriorated because of the lack of funding, staffing and maintenance. The challenges with WIP are numerous and complicated.

We appreciate having the opportunity address the following specific and time sensitive matters with you: (1) the critical need for a project engineer to lead the Wapato Irrigation Project, (2) the lack of ready access to engineering support to the Wapato Irrigation Project personnel, (3) the need for better mid-level management and training, (4) numerous issues of years of deferred maintenance, (5) employee safety and health issues, (6) the need to address employee hiring and retention issues to compete with neighboring irrigation projects for the best employees, (7) the use of infrared cameras to identify problems while the equipment is under full load as a preventative maintenance tool; (8) needed support of Senate Bill 715 as a means to fund improvements to the infrastructure, and (9) Toppenish Creek pump house tort claims.

The Board feels it is imperative that these issues be addressed in a timely fashion and would appreciate any assistance you may be able to provide in order for the Wapato Irrigation Project to accomplish them.

Sincerely,

Lon K. Inaba
President

_____

RESPONSE TO WRITTEN QUESTIONS SUBMITTED BY HON. JOHN MCCAIN TO
LARRY ROBERTS

Mr. Roberts, the Colorado River Indian Tribes Irrigation project is one of the oldest in the country, and like the other projects we heard about from the witnesses, it has been dramatically underfunded. One unique feature about the CRIT Irrigation project, however, is that it also includes a Bureau of Reclamation hydroelectric dam which was built into the system in the 1940s. The BIA collects revenues for the tribe from this generation facility in an interest generating "385(c)" account, but the funds can only be used for limited purposes such as repairs to the dam. The rules prohibit expenditures even though the account balance is more than adequate to ensure that even catastrophic maintenance needs are met.

Provided there were provisions which required that the account maintain a sufficient balance to meet all routine and catastrophic maintenance needs, would the Department support legislation to allow the Tribe to spend a small portion of that money, such as the interest generated by the account, on self-determination projects such as creating a Department of Energy to help administer water and power distribution programs?

Response: The Department is supportive of tribal self-determination and would be willing to work with Senator McCain and the Senate Committee on Indian Affairs to further consider expanded uses of these funds and potentially craft appropriate legislation.